# Ethiopian Orthodox Bible

Unveiling the Detailed History of the Oldest Surviving Bible with 88 Books including Apocrypha

Biblia Print

**Copyright © 2024 by Biblia Print**

*All rights reserved. No part of this book may be reproduced, stored in a retrieval system, or transmitted in any form or by any means, electronic, mechanical, photocopying, recording, or otherwise, without prior written permission from the author, except for brief quotations in critical reviews or article.*

# Table of Contents

**Introduction**     **1**

**Chapter 1**     **12**

**Tracing the Roots: Early Manuscripts and Cultural Influences**     **12**

    The Origins of the Ethiopian Orthodox Church     13

    Historical Manuscripts and Their Preservation     15

    Cultural Influences Shaping the Bible's Development 17

**Chapter 2**     **22**

**Formation of the Canon: The Unique 88 Books**     **22**

    The Process of Canonization in the Ethiopian Orthodox Tradition     23

    Key Figures and Events in the Formation of the Canon     25

    Comparisons with Other Christian Canons     27

    The Process of Canonization in the Ethiopian Orthodox Tradition     31

    Key Figures and Events in the Formation of the Canon     33

    Comparisons with Other Christian Canons     35

    Cultural Influences Shaping the Bible's Development 39

**Chapter 3**     **44**

**Unveiling the Apocrypha: History and Significance 44**

    Definition and Historical Context of the Apocrypha 45

    The Spiritual and Theological Value of the Apocrypha     49

| | |
|---|---|
| **Chapter 4** | **54** |
| **Exploring Apocryphal Books: Tobit and Judith** | **54** |
| Historical and Literary Analysis of Tobit | 54 |
| Historical and Literary Analysis of Judith | 58 |
| Their Roles within Ethiopian Orthodox Tradition | 61 |
| **Chapter 5** | **64** |
| **Exploring Apocryphal Books: 1 and 2 Maccabees** | **64** |
| Historical Context and Significance of 1 Maccabees | 64 |
| Historical Context and Significance of 2 Maccabees | 67 |
| Their Roles Within Ethiopian Orthodox Tradition | 70 |
| **Chapter 6** | **73** |
| **Exploring Apocryphal Books: Wisdom of Solomon and Ecclesiasticus** | **73** |
| Historical and Literary Analysis of Wisdom of Solomon | 73 |
| Historical and Literary Analysis of Ecclesiasticus (Sirach) | 75 |
| Their Roles within Ethiopian Orthodox Tradition | 76 |
| **Chapter 7** | **80** |
| **Exploring Apocryphal Books: Baruch** | **80** |
| Historical and Literary Analysis of Baruch | 80 |
| Its Role within Ethiopian Orthodox Tradition | 82 |
| **Chapter 8** | **87** |
| **The Old Testament: Foundations of Faith** | **87** |
| Overview of the Old Testament Books | 87 |
| Historical Context, Literary Genres, and Theological Themes | 90 |

Unique Features in the Ethiopian Orthodox Old
Testament 93

## Chapter 9 — 98
### The New Testament: The Life and Teachings of Christ — 98

Overview of the New Testament Books 98

Historical Context, Literary Genres, and Theological Themes 101

Unique Features in the Ethiopian Orthodox New Testament 105

## Chapter 10 — 110
### The Pseudepigrapha: Expanding the Canon — 110

Introduction to the Pseudepigrapha 110

Historical and Literary Analysis of Key Books 112

Their Influence on Ancient Judaism and Christianity 118

## Chapter 11 — 123
### Influence on Ethiopian Society — 123

The Bible's Role in Shaping Ethiopian Social Structures 123

Influence on Laws, Customs, and Daily Life 125

## Chapter 12 — 133
### Art, Music, and Identity — 133

The Impact of the Bible on Ethiopian Art 133

Influence on Traditional and Contemporary Ethiopian Music 137

The Bible's Role in Forging Ethiopian Identity 141

## Chapter 13 — 146
### Historical Disputes Over Canonicity — 146

Historical Debates Within the Church 146

Comparisons with Canonicity Disputes in Other Traditions — 150

## Chapter 14 — 155
## Modern Interpretive Debates — 155

Contemporary Theological and Scholarly Debates — 155

The Impact of Modern Scholarship on Traditional Beliefs — 161

## Chapter 15 — 168
## Efforts to Digitize and Increase Accessibility — 168

Projects and Initiatives to Preserve and Digitize Manuscripts — 168

Efforts to Make the Ethiopian Orthodox Bible Accessible to a Global Audience — 173

## Chapter 16 — 179
## Spiritual Wisdom and Insights — 179

Key Spiritual Teachings and Insights from the Ethiopian Orthodox Bible — 179

The Relevance of These Teachings in Contemporary Life — 185

## Chapter 17 — 192
## Historical Significance and Scholarly Importance — 192

The Bible's Status as the Oldest Surviving Bible — 192

Its Importance for Scholars of Religion, History, and Culture — 198

## Chapter 18 — 205
## Liturgical Celebrations and Manuscript Illumination — 205

The Role of the Bible in Ethiopian Liturgical Practices — 205

The Art and Significance of Illuminated Manuscripts
211
**Chapter 19**     **219**
**Shaping Ethiopian Identity and Spirituality**     **219**
The Bible's Enduring Influence on Ethiopian Identity
219

The Role of Scripture in Ethiopian Spirituality and
Religious Practices     225
**Conclusion**     **231**

# Introduction

In the annals of religious history, few texts hold as much intrigue, mystery, and cultural significance as the Ethiopian Orthodox Bible. This sacred tome, revered by millions, stands as the oldest surviving Bible, a testament to a rich and unbroken spiritual tradition that has endured for centuries. With its 88 books, including the Apocrypha, the Ethiopian Orthodox Bible offers a unique and expansive canon that sets it apart from its Western counterparts. This introduction aims to provide an overview of this extraordinary text, exploring its origins, development, and the profound impact it has had on Ethiopian culture and beyond.

The Ethiopian Orthodox Church, one of the oldest Christian denominations, traces its roots back to the early centuries of Christianity. According to tradition, Christianity was introduced to Ethiopia by St. Frumentius in the 4th century, under the reign of King Ezana. The adoption of Christianity as the state religion marked the beginning of a deep and enduring relationship between the Ethiopian people and their faith. Over the centuries, the Ethiopian Orthodox Bible emerged as a cornerstone of this relationship, reflecting the theological, cultural, and historical milieu of the Ethiopian Christian experience.

What distinguishes the Ethiopian Orthodox Bible is its unique composition. While the Protestant Bible contains 66 books, the Ethiopian Orthodox Bible includes an additional 22 books, bringing the total to 88. These extra books, encompassing the Apocrypha and the Pseudepigrapha, provide a broader and more diverse theological perspective. The Apocrypha, a collection of texts not included in the Hebrew Bible but considered canonical by the Ethiopian Orthodox Church, offers rich narratives and spiritual insights. Similarly, the Pseudepigrapha, a group of ancient Jewish writings attributed to various biblical figures, adds depth and context to the biblical narrative.

The inclusion of these additional texts is not merely a matter of historical curiosity; it is a reflection of the

Ethiopian Orthodox Church's theological worldview. For Ethiopian Christians, the Bible is not just a collection of sacred writings but a living document that speaks to the entirety of human experience. The stories, laws, prophecies, and teachings contained within its pages are seen as divinely inspired, providing guidance and wisdom for all aspects of life.

The Ethiopian Orthodox Bible's 88 books offer a comprehensive and nuanced understanding of the biblical narrative. This expanded canon includes texts that provide historical context, spiritual guidance, and moral teachings, all of which are integral to the Ethiopian Orthodox faith. The significance of these books lies not only in their content but also in their historical and cultural context. Each book reflects a specific aspect of the Ethiopian Christian tradition, contributing to a rich tapestry of faith and practice.

Among the additional texts included in the Ethiopian Orthodox Bible are the seven books of the Apocrypha: Tobit, Judith, 1 Maccabees, 2 Maccabees, Wisdom of

Solomon, Ecclesiasticus (Sirach), and Baruch. These books, while not part of the Hebrew Bible, hold a special place in the Ethiopian Orthodox tradition. For instance, the book of Tobit is valued for its teachings on righteousness, charity, and the importance of family. Judith, a powerful narrative of faith and courage, serves as an inspirational tale of divine intervention and deliverance. The Maccabees books recount the struggles and triumphs of the Jewish people during the Maccabean Revolt, highlighting themes of perseverance and divine justice.

The Wisdom of Solomon and Ecclesiasticus, also known as Sirach, are revered for their profound philosophical and ethical teachings. These books offer insights into the nature of wisdom, justice, and the human condition, providing timeless guidance for personal and communal conduct. Baruch, traditionally attributed to the secretary of the prophet Jeremiah, emphasizes themes of repentance, hope, and divine mercy, resonating deeply with the Ethiopian Orthodox emphasis on spiritual renewal and redemption.

In addition to the Apocrypha, the Ethiopian Orthodox Bible includes 15 books of the Pseudepigrapha. These texts, which include works such as 1 Enoch, Jubilees, and the Testaments of the Twelve Patriarchs, offer a rich and varied perspective on biblical history and theology. 1 Enoch, for example, provides a detailed account of the fallen angels, the flood, and the final judgment, themes that are echoed in the New Testament. Jubilees, also known as "Little Genesis," offers a retelling of biblical history from creation to the giving of the Law at Sinai, emphasizing the importance of covenant and divine providence. The Testaments of the Twelve Patriarchs, a collection of ethical teachings attributed to the twelve sons of Jacob, provide moral and spiritual guidance, reflecting the values and beliefs of ancient Jewish and Christian communities.

The inclusion of these additional texts in the Ethiopian Orthodox Bible is a testament to the church's commitment to preserving and transmitting a comprehensive and holistic understanding of the biblical narrative. Each book, with its unique themes and teachings, contributes to a broader and more nuanced theological framework, enriching the spiritual and intellectual life of the Ethiopian Orthodox community.

The structure of the Ethiopian Orthodox Bible reflects its diverse and multifaceted nature. The Bible is traditionally divided into several sections, each with its own distinct focus and purpose. These sections include the Pentateuch (the first five books of Moses), the Historical Books, the Wisdom Literature, the Prophets, the Gospels, the Acts of the Apostles, the Epistles, and the Apocryphal and Pseudepigraphal writings. Each section serves to illuminate different aspects of the divine narrative, providing a comprehensive and integrated account of God's relationship with humanity.

The Pentateuch, also known as the Torah, forms the foundation of the biblical narrative. These five books – Genesis, Exodus, Leviticus, Numbers, and Deuteronomy – recount the creation of the world, the origins of humanity, and the establishment of God's covenant with the people of Israel. These texts are central to the Ethiopian Orthodox faith, emphasizing themes of creation, covenant, law, and divine providence.

The Historical Books, which include texts such as Joshua, Judges, Samuel, and Kings, provide a detailed account of the history of Israel from the conquest of Canaan to the Babylonian exile. These books highlight the faithfulness of God and the consequences of obedience and disobedience to His covenant. They also underscore the importance of leadership, justice, and the pursuit of righteousness in the life of the community.

The Wisdom Literature, encompassing books such as Psalms, Proverbs, Job, and Ecclesiastes, offers profound insights into the nature of wisdom, suffering, and the human condition. These texts are cherished for their poetic beauty and philosophical depth, providing timeless guidance for personal and communal conduct. The Psalms, in particular, hold a special place in Ethiopian Orthodox worship, serving as a rich source of liturgical and devotional material.

The Prophets, including major and minor prophetic books, convey the messages of God's spokesmen to the people of Israel. These texts, which include Isaiah, Jeremiah, Ezekiel, and the Twelve Minor Prophets, emphasize themes of judgment, repentance, and hope. They call the people to faithfulness and justice, warning of the consequences of disobedience and promising restoration and redemption for those who turn to God.

The Gospels – Matthew, Mark, Luke, and John – form the heart of the New Testament, recounting the life, teachings, death, and resurrection of Jesus Christ. These texts are central to the Christian faith, emphasizing the themes of salvation, grace, and the Kingdom of God. The Acts of the Apostles continues the narrative, detailing the spread of the early church and the work of the Holy Spirit in the lives of the apostles and early Christians.

The Epistles, letters written by apostles such as Paul, Peter, James, and John, provide theological instruction and practical guidance for the early Christian communities. These texts address a wide range of issues, from doctrine and ethics to church organization and personal conduct, reflecting the diverse and dynamic nature of the early Christian movement.

The Apocryphal and Pseudepigraphal writings, as previously discussed, offer additional perspectives and insights into the biblical narrative. These texts, while not included in the Protestant canon, are considered divinely inspired and authoritative within the Ethiopian Orthodox tradition. They provide valuable historical, theological, and ethical teachings, enriching the overall understanding of the Bible and its message.

The themes of the Ethiopian Orthodox Bible are as diverse and multifaceted as its contents. Central to these themes is the concept of covenant – the relationship between God and humanity, established through divine promises and human response. This theme is woven throughout the biblical narrative, from the covenant with

Noah and Abraham to the new covenant established through Jesus Christ.

Another key theme is the idea of divine providence – the belief that God is actively involved in the world, guiding and sustaining His creation. This theme is evident in the stories of the patriarchs, the history of Israel, the teachings of the prophets, and the life and ministry of Jesus. It underscores the faithfulness of God and the importance of trust and obedience in the life of the believer.

The themes of judgment and redemption are also central to the Ethiopian Orthodox Bible. The prophets, in particular, emphasize the consequences of sin and disobedience, warning of divine judgment and calling for repentance. At the same time, they offer the hope of redemption and restoration for those who turn to God in faith and obedience. This dual theme of judgment and redemption is ultimately fulfilled in the life, death, and resurrection of Jesus Christ, who offers salvation and eternal life to all who believe in Him.

Finally, the Ethiopian Orthodox Bible emphasizes the importance of wisdom and righteousness in the life of the believer. The Wisdom Literature, in particular, provides profound insights into the nature of wisdom, justice, and the human condition. It calls believers to pursue righteousness, seek justice, and live in accordance with God's will, reflecting His character and values in their daily lives.

The Ethiopian Orthodox Bible stands as a timeless treasure, a rich and multifaceted testament to the faith, wisdom, and resilience of the Ethiopian Christian tradition. Its unique composition, profound themes, and deep cultural significance make it a vital and enduring part of the spiritual heritage of Ethiopia and the wider Christian community. As we delve into the detailed history and significance of this remarkable text, we gain a deeper appreciation for its role in shaping the faith, identity, and culture of the Ethiopian people, and its enduring relevance for believers around the world.

# Chapter 1

# Tracing the Roots: Early Manuscripts and Cultural Influences

The Ethiopian Orthodox Church stands as a beacon of ancient Christian tradition, with roots that trace back to the early centuries of Christianity. Its unique history and development are closely tied to the broader story of the Ethiopian Orthodox Bible, a text that not only serves as a religious cornerstone but also as a cultural artifact that has shaped the identity and heritage of the Ethiopian people. Understanding the origins of the Ethiopian Orthodox Church, the historical manuscripts that have been preserved over centuries, and the cultural influences that have shaped the Bible's development provides a rich tapestry of history, faith, and resilience.

# The Origins of the Ethiopian Orthodox Church

The Ethiopian Orthodox Church, also known as the Ethiopian Orthodox Tewahedo Church, is one of the oldest Christian denominations in the world. Its origins are traditionally linked to the conversion of the Ethiopian Kingdom of Aksum in the 4th century. According to historical accounts, Christianity was introduced to Ethiopia by Saint Frumentius, who was later consecrated as the first Bishop of Aksum by Athanasius of Alexandria. This early adoption of Christianity by the Ethiopian monarchy marked the beginning of a profound and enduring relationship between the Ethiopian people and their faith.

The story of Saint Frumentius and his brother Aedesius is a tale of providence and divine mission. Captured as boys during a voyage on the Red Sea, they were brought to the royal court in Aksum. There, they gained favor with the king and were eventually entrusted with positions of influence. Upon the king's death, Frumentius, with the queen's support, began to promote

Christianity among the Aksumites. His efforts bore fruit, and by the time he traveled to Alexandria to seek a bishopric for Ethiopia, the seeds of Christianity had firmly taken root. Athanasius, recognizing the potential for a new Christian stronghold, consecrated Frumentius as Bishop of Aksum, bestowing upon him the task of nurturing the fledgling church.

The conversion of the Ethiopian kingdom was not merely a political or social transformation but a deeply spiritual and cultural shift. The adoption of Christianity brought with it a new worldview, a new set of values, and a new way of life. The Ethiopian Orthodox Church developed its own unique traditions, liturgies, and theological perspectives, distinct yet deeply connected to the wider Christian world. This early foundation set the stage for the development of the Ethiopian Orthodox Bible, a text that would come to embody the spiritual and cultural heritage of the Ethiopian people.

# Historical Manuscripts and Their Preservation

The preservation of historical manuscripts has been a vital aspect of the Ethiopian Orthodox Church's commitment to safeguarding its religious and cultural heritage. The Ethiopian Orthodox Bible, with its 88 books, is a testament to this enduring dedication. These manuscripts, many of which are written in Ge'ez, the ancient liturgical language of Ethiopia, are housed in monasteries, churches, and libraries across the country. They represent a rich and varied collection of biblical texts, theological treatises, liturgical works, and historical records, each contributing to the understanding of the church's history and doctrine.

One of the most significant collections of Ethiopian manuscripts is found in the monastery of Debre Damo, located in the Tigray region. This ancient monastery, perched atop a sheer cliff, is accessible only by climbing a rope, a testament to the monks' commitment to preserving their sacred texts from potential invaders or natural disasters. The manuscripts housed at Debre

Damo include some of the oldest known copies of the Ethiopian Orthodox Bible, along with other important religious and historical texts.

The preservation of these manuscripts has not been without challenges. Over the centuries, Ethiopia has faced invasions, wars, and internal strife, all of which have threatened the survival of its cultural and religious heritage. Yet, despite these adversities, the Ethiopian Orthodox Church has remained steadfast in its efforts to protect and preserve its sacred texts. Monasteries and churches have served as sanctuaries for these manuscripts, ensuring their survival through turbulent times. The dedication of the Ethiopian clergy and laity to the preservation of their spiritual heritage is a testament to the enduring importance of these texts in the life of the church and the broader Ethiopian society.

In recent years, efforts have been made to digitize these ancient manuscripts, making them more accessible to scholars and the public while ensuring their preservation for future generations. Organizations such as the

Ethiopian Manuscript Microfilm Library (EMML) have played a crucial role in these efforts, photographing and cataloging thousands of manuscripts from across the country. These digital archives provide a valuable resource for researchers and help to protect the fragile originals from the wear and tear of handling.

## Cultural Influences Shaping the Bible's Development

The development of the Ethiopian Orthodox Bible has been influenced by a variety of cultural, historical, and religious factors. One of the most significant influences has been the ancient Judaic traditions that were present in Ethiopia prior to the introduction of Christianity. The Ethiopian Orthodox Church has long held that the Queen of Sheba, who visited King Solomon in Jerusalem, established a connection between Ethiopia and the Hebrew faith. This connection is reflected in the Ethiopian Orthodox Bible, which includes several books of the Hebrew Scriptures, as well as texts that are unique to the Ethiopian canon, such as the Book of Enoch and the Book of Jubilees.

The influence of Judaic traditions is evident in the Ethiopian Orthodox Church's liturgical practices, calendar, and dietary laws, all of which bear a resemblance to ancient Jewish customs. This blending of Judaic and Christian elements has given the Ethiopian Orthodox faith a distinctive character, one that is deeply rooted in the ancient traditions of both Judaism and Christianity.

Another significant cultural influence on the development of the Ethiopian Orthodox Bible is the rich literary and artistic heritage of Ethiopia. The illuminated manuscripts of the Ethiopian Orthodox Bible are renowned for their intricate and colorful illustrations, which depict biblical scenes, saints, and religious symbols. These artworks are not merely decorative but serve as a visual interpretation of the biblical narrative, enhancing the spiritual and educational value of the text. The tradition of manuscript illumination in Ethiopia dates back to the early centuries of Christianity and has been preserved and developed over the centuries by generations of skilled scribes and artists.

The Ethiopian Orthodox Bible has also been shaped by the church's interactions with other Christian traditions, particularly the Coptic Church of Egypt. The Ethiopian Orthodox Church was historically part of the Coptic Orthodox Church, sharing a common theological and liturgical heritage. This connection is reflected in the Ethiopian Orthodox Bible, which includes texts and traditions that are also found in the Coptic tradition. The influence of the Coptic Church is evident in the theological writings, liturgical texts, and ecclesiastical art of the Ethiopian Orthodox Church, contributing to the rich and diverse heritage of the Ethiopian Orthodox Bible.

The cultural and historical context of Ethiopia has also played a crucial role in shaping the Ethiopian Orthodox Bible. Ethiopia's unique geographical location, at the crossroads of Africa, the Middle East, and the

Mediterranean, has made it a melting pot of cultural and religious influences. Over the centuries, Ethiopia has been influenced by various civilizations, including the Egyptians, Greeks, Romans, and Arabs, all of whom have left their mark on Ethiopian culture and religion. This diverse cultural heritage is reflected in the Ethiopian Orthodox Bible, which incorporates elements from various traditions and civilizations, creating a unique and comprehensive spiritual text.

The Ethiopian Orthodox Bible is not just a religious text but a living document that reflects the spiritual, cultural, and historical identity of the Ethiopian people. It is a testament to the enduring faith, resilience, and creativity of the Ethiopian Orthodox Church and its followers. As we trace the roots of the Ethiopian Orthodox Bible, we gain a deeper appreciation for its unique composition, profound themes, and cultural significance. This ancient text continues to inspire and guide the Ethiopian Orthodox faithful, providing a rich and enduring legacy for future generations.

The Ethiopian Orthodox Bible is a timeless treasure, a rich and multifaceted testament to the faith, wisdom, and resilience of the Ethiopian Christian tradition. Its unique composition, profound themes, and deep cultural significance make it a vital and enduring part of the spiritual heritage of Ethiopia and the wider Christian community. As we explore the detailed history and significance of this remarkable text, we gain a deeper appreciation for its role in shaping the faith, identity, and culture of the Ethiopian people, and its enduring relevance for believers around the world.

# Chapter 2

# Formation of the Canon: The Unique 88 Books

The formation of the Ethiopian Orthodox Bible canon, with its unique composition of 88 books, is a story of faith, tradition, and cultural evolution. The process of canonization within the Ethiopian Orthodox tradition is a testament to the church's distinct identity and its reverence for sacred texts that provide spiritual guidance, historical context, and theological depth. This chapter explores the journey of the Ethiopian Orthodox Bible's canonization, key figures and events that played pivotal roles, and comparisons with other Christian canons to highlight the unique aspects of the Ethiopian scriptural tradition.

# The Process of Canonization in the Ethiopian Orthodox Tradition

Canonization, the process by which a set of texts is deemed authoritative and divinely inspired, has been a complex and nuanced journey in the Ethiopian Orthodox Church. Unlike the relatively more standardized processes seen in Western Christianity, the Ethiopian canonization process was heavily influenced by local traditions, cultural context, and the early Christian connections to Judaism.

In the Ethiopian Orthodox tradition, the canonization of scriptures began with the recognition of texts that were used liturgically and theologically significant within the community. This process was less about formal decrees and more about organic development over centuries. The Ethiopian Orthodox Church's close relationship with the Coptic Church of Alexandria played a significant role in the early formation of its biblical canon. Many of the texts considered canonical in Ethiopia were also revered in the early Alexandrian Christian tradition.

The Ethiopian Orthodox Bible includes all the books found in the traditional Christian Bible, but it expands further to include books that are considered apocryphal or pseudepigraphal in other traditions. These additional books reflect the Ethiopian Church's broader understanding of sacred scripture, which encompasses texts that provide moral instruction, historical narratives, and apocalyptic visions. This inclusive approach to scripture is rooted in the church's mission to preserve and transmit a comprehensive spiritual heritage that reflects the fullness of God's revelation to humanity.

The process of canonization was also influenced by the cultural and religious context of Ethiopia. The Ethiopian Orthodox Church's connection to ancient Judaism, as seen in the inclusion of texts like the Book of Enoch and the Book of Jubilees, reflects the church's desire to maintain a continuity with the Jewish roots of Christianity. This connection is further emphasized by the presence of the Old Testament apocryphal books, which were widely read and respected in early Jewish communities.

## Key Figures and Events in the Formation of the Canon

Several key figures and events have been instrumental in shaping the Ethiopian Orthodox Bible's canon. One of the most significant figures is Saint Frumentius, known as Abba Selama, who played a crucial role in the early establishment of Christianity in Ethiopia. As the first bishop of Aksum, Frumentius was not only a spiritual leader but also a cultural bridge, helping to integrate Christian texts into the Ethiopian religious landscape. His influence ensured that the nascent Ethiopian Christian community had access to a wide range of sacred writings.

Another pivotal event in the formation of the canon was the Council of Nicea in 325 AD. While the council itself did not directly impact the Ethiopian canon, it marked a period of increased communication and interaction between the Ethiopian Church and other Christian communities. This interaction facilitated the exchange of texts and theological ideas, contributing to the expansion of the Ethiopian scriptural collection.

The translation of the Bible into Ge'ez, the ancient liturgical language of Ethiopia, was another landmark event. This monumental task, undertaken by early Ethiopian scholars, was crucial for the establishment of a canonical text that was accessible to the Ethiopian faithful. The translation process was meticulous, ensuring that the theological nuances and spiritual depth of the original texts were preserved. This translation project not only made the scriptures accessible but also reinforced the distinct identity of the Ethiopian Orthodox Church.

Throughout the centuries, Ethiopian monastic communities have played a vital role in preserving and transmitting the canonical texts. Monasteries such as Debre Damo and Debre Libanos have been centers of learning and manuscript production, safeguarding the sacred texts through turbulent times. The monks' dedication to copying and preserving these texts ensured that the Ethiopian canon remained intact and accessible to future generations.

# Comparisons with Other Christian Canons

The Ethiopian Orthodox Bible stands out for its unique composition of 88 books, a significantly larger canon compared to other Christian traditions. For example, the Protestant Bible contains 66 books, the Roman Catholic Bible includes 73 books, and the Eastern Orthodox Bible has a slightly varying number of books depending on the tradition, but generally includes around 78 books. These differences highlight the diverse approaches to canonization within Christianity and the particular historical and theological contexts that shaped each tradition's canon.

One of the most notable differences is the inclusion of the Old Testament Apocrypha and Pseudepigrapha in the Ethiopian canon. These books, such as Tobit, Judith, and 1 Enoch, are considered canonical and divinely inspired within the Ethiopian Orthodox Church. In contrast, these texts are often relegated to the status of deuterocanonical (secondary canon) or apocryphal (non-canonical) in other traditions. The Ethiopian Church's inclusion of these texts reflects its broader understanding of scripture and its commitment to preserving a rich and diverse spiritual heritage.

The Ethiopian Orthodox Bible also includes unique texts that are not found in other Christian canons. The Book of Enoch, for instance, is a prominent part of the Ethiopian canon but is not considered canonical by most other Christian traditions. This ancient text, attributed to the patriarch Enoch, provides valuable insights into early Jewish and Christian apocalyptic literature. Its inclusion in the Ethiopian canon underscores the church's connection to ancient Judaic traditions and its desire to preserve a comprehensive scriptural heritage.

Another significant aspect of the Ethiopian canon is the inclusion of the Books of the Covenant, a collection of texts that outline the ethical and moral teachings of the church. These texts, which include the Didache and the Apostolic Constitutions, provide practical guidance for the Christian life and reflect the Ethiopian Church's emphasis on ethical living and community cohesion.

The formation of the Ethiopian Orthodox Bible's canon is also distinguished by its historical continuity. While many other Christian traditions have undergone significant changes and debates over their canons, the Ethiopian Orthodox Church has maintained a relatively stable and consistent canon over the centuries. This stability is a testament to the church's deep reverence for its sacred texts and its commitment to preserving its spiritual heritage.

The process of canonization in the Ethiopian Orthodox tradition was influenced by a variety of cultural, historical, and religious factors. The early adoption of Christianity by the Ethiopian monarchy, the translation of the Bible into Ge'ez, and the dedication of monastic communities to preserving sacred texts all played crucial roles in shaping the Ethiopian canon. The Ethiopian Orthodox Bible's unique composition of 88 books reflects the church's inclusive approach to scripture and its commitment to preserving a comprehensive spiritual heritage.

In comparison with other Christian canons, the Ethiopian Orthodox Bible stands out for its inclusion of the Old Testament Apocrypha and Pseudepigrapha, as well as unique texts like the Book of Enoch and the Books of the Covenant. These differences highlight the diverse approaches to canonization within Christianity and the particular historical and theological contexts that shaped each tradition's canon. The Ethiopian Orthodox Church's commitment to preserving a rich and diverse scriptural heritage has ensured that its canon remains a vital and enduring part of its spiritual and cultural identity.

The formation of the Ethiopian Orthodox Bible's canon is a testament to the faith, resilience, and dedication of the Ethiopian Orthodox Church and its followers. This unique and comprehensive canon continues to inspire and guide the Ethiopian Orthodox faithful, providing a rich and enduring legacy for future generations. As we explore the detailed history and significance of this remarkable text, we gain a deeper appreciation for its role in shaping the faith, identity, and culture of the

Ethiopian people, and its enduring relevance for believers around the world.

## The Process of Canonization in the Ethiopian Orthodox Tradition

Canonization, the process by which a set of texts is deemed authoritative and divinely inspired, has been a complex and nuanced journey in the Ethiopian Orthodox Church. Unlike the relatively more standardized processes seen in Western Christianity, the Ethiopian canonization process was heavily influenced by local traditions, cultural context, and the early Christian connections to Judaism.

In the Ethiopian Orthodox tradition, the canonization of scriptures began with the recognition of texts that were used liturgically and theologically significant within the community. This process was less about formal decrees and more about organic development over centuries. The Ethiopian Orthodox Church's close relationship with the Coptic Church of Alexandria played a significant role in the early formation of its biblical canon. Many of the texts considered canonical in Ethiopia were also revered in the early Alexandrian Christian tradition.

The Ethiopian Orthodox Bible includes all the books found in the traditional Christian Bible, but it expands further to include books that are considered apocryphal or pseudepigraphal in other traditions. These additional books reflect the Ethiopian Church's broader understanding of sacred scripture, which encompasses texts that provide moral instruction, historical narratives, and apocalyptic visions. This inclusive approach to scripture is rooted in the church's mission to preserve and transmit a comprehensive spiritual heritage that reflects the fullness of God's revelation to humanity.

The process of canonization was also influenced by the cultural and religious context of Ethiopia. The Ethiopian Orthodox Church's connection to ancient Judaism, as seen in the inclusion of texts like the Book of Enoch and the Book of Jubilees, reflects the church's desire to maintain a continuity with the Jewish roots of Christianity. This connection is further emphasized by the presence of the Old Testament apocryphal books, which were widely read and respected in early Jewish communities.

## Key Figures and Events in the Formation of the Canon

Several key figures and events have been instrumental in shaping the Ethiopian Orthodox Bible's canon. One of the most significant figures is Saint Frumentius, known as Abba Selama, who played a crucial role in the early establishment of Christianity in Ethiopia. As the first bishop of Aksum, Frumentius was not only a spiritual leader but also a cultural bridge, helping to integrate Christian texts into the Ethiopian religious landscape. His influence ensured that the nascent Ethiopian Christian community had access to a wide range of sacred writings.

Another pivotal event in the formation of the canon was the Council of Nicea in 325 AD. While the council itself did not directly impact the Ethiopian canon, it marked a period of increased communication and interaction between the Ethiopian Church and other Christian communities. This interaction facilitated the exchange of texts and theological ideas, contributing to the expansion of the Ethiopian scriptural collection.

The translation of the Bible into Ge'ez, the ancient liturgical language of Ethiopia, was another landmark event. This monumental task, undertaken by early Ethiopian scholars, was crucial for the establishment of a canonical text that was accessible to the Ethiopian faithful. The translation process was meticulous, ensuring that the theological nuances and spiritual depth of the original texts were preserved. This translation project not only made the scriptures accessible but also reinforced the distinct identity of the Ethiopian Orthodox Church.

Throughout the centuries, Ethiopian monastic communities have played a vital role in preserving and transmitting the canonical texts. Monasteries such as Debre Damo and Debre Libanos have been centers of learning and manuscript production, safeguarding the sacred texts through turbulent times. The monks' dedication to copying and preserving these texts ensured that the Ethiopian canon remained intact and accessible to future generations.

## Comparisons with Other Christian Canons

The Ethiopian Orthodox Bible stands out for its unique composition of 88 books, a significantly larger canon compared to other Christian traditions. For example, the Protestant Bible contains 66 books, the Roman Catholic Bible includes 73 books, and the Eastern Orthodox Bible has a slightly varying number of books depending on the tradition, but generally includes around 78 books. These differences highlight the diverse approaches to canonization within Christianity and the particular historical and theological contexts that shaped each tradition's canon.

One of the most notable differences is the inclusion of the Old Testament Apocrypha and Pseudepigrapha in the Ethiopian canon. These books, such as Tobit, Judith, and

1 Enoch, are considered canonical and divinely inspired within the Ethiopian Orthodox Church. In contrast, these texts are often relegated to the status of deuterocanonical (secondary canon) or apocryphal (non-canonical) in other traditions. The Ethiopian Church's inclusion of these texts reflects its broader understanding of scripture and its commitment to preserving a rich and diverse spiritual heritage.

The Ethiopian Orthodox Bible also includes unique texts that are not found in other Christian canons. The Book of Enoch, for instance, is a prominent part of the Ethiopian canon but is not considered canonical by most other Christian traditions. This ancient text, attributed to the patriarch Enoch, provides valuable insights into early Jewish and Christian apocalyptic literature. Its inclusion in the Ethiopian canon underscores the church's connection to ancient Judaic traditions and its desire to preserve a comprehensive scriptural heritage.

Another significant aspect of the Ethiopian canon is the inclusion of the Books of the Covenant, a collection of texts that outline the ethical and moral teachings of the church. These texts, which include the Didache and the Apostolic Constitutions, provide practical guidance for the Christian life and reflect the Ethiopian Church's emphasis on ethical living and community cohesion.

The formation of the Ethiopian Orthodox Bible's canon is also distinguished by its historical continuity. While many other Christian traditions have undergone significant changes and debates over their canons, the Ethiopian Orthodox Church has maintained a relatively stable and consistent canon over the centuries. This stability is a testament to the church's deep reverence for its sacred texts and its commitment to preserving its spiritual heritage.

The process of canonization in the Ethiopian Orthodox tradition was influenced by a variety of cultural, historical, and religious factors. The early adoption of Christianity by the Ethiopian monarchy, the translation of the Bible into Ge'ez, and the dedication of monastic communities to preserving sacred texts all played crucial roles in shaping the Ethiopian canon. The Ethiopian Orthodox Bible's unique composition of 88 books reflects the church's inclusive approach to scripture and its commitment to preserving a comprehensive spiritual heritage.

In comparison with other Christian canons, the Ethiopian Orthodox Bible stands out for its inclusion of the Old Testament Apocrypha and Pseudepigrapha, as well as unique texts like the Book of Enoch and the Books of the Covenant. These differences highlight the diverse approaches to canonization within Christianity and the particular historical and theological contexts that shaped each tradition's canon. The Ethiopian Orthodox Church's commitment to preserving a rich and diverse scriptural heritage has ensured that its canon remains a vital and enduring part of its spiritual and cultural identity.

The formation of the Ethiopian Orthodox Bible's canon is a testament to the faith, resilience, and dedication of the Ethiopian Orthodox Church and its followers. This unique and comprehensive canon continues to inspire and guide the Ethiopian Orthodox faithful, providing a rich and enduring legacy for future generations. As we explore the detailed history and significance of this remarkable text, we gain a deeper appreciation for its role in shaping the faith, identity, and culture of the Ethiopian people, and its enduring relevance for believers around the world.

## Cultural Influences Shaping the Bible's Development

The development of the Ethiopian Orthodox Bible has been influenced by a variety of cultural, historical, and religious factors. One of the most significant influences has been the ancient Judaic traditions that were present in Ethiopia prior to the introduction of Christianity. The Ethiopian Orthodox Church has long held that the Queen of Sheba, who visited King Solomon in Jerusalem, established a connection between Ethiopia and the Hebrew faith. This connection is reflected in the Ethiopian Orthodox Bible, which includes several books of the Hebrew Scriptures, as well as texts that are unique to the Ethiopian canon, such as the Book of Enoch and the Book of Jubilees.

The influence of Judaic traditions is evident in the Ethiopian Orthodox Church's liturgical practices, calendar, and dietary laws, all of which bear a resemblance to ancient Jewish customs. This blending of Judaic and Christian elements has given the Ethiopian Orthodox faith a distinctive character, one that is deeply rooted in the ancient traditions of both Judaism and Christianity.

Another significant cultural influence on the development of the Ethiopian Orthodox Bible is the rich literary and artistic heritage of Ethiopia. The illuminated manuscripts of the Ethiopian Orthodox Bible are renowned for their intricate and colorful illustrations, which depict biblical scenes, saints, and religious symbols. These artworks are not merely decorative but serve as a visual interpretation of the biblical narrative, enhancing the spiritual and educational value of the text. The tradition of manuscript illumination in Ethiopia dates back to the early centuries of Christianity and has been preserved and developed over the centuries by generations of skilled scribes and artists.

The Ethiopian Orthodox Bible has also been shaped by the church's interactions with other Christian traditions, particularly the Coptic Church of Egypt. The Ethiopian Orthodox Church was historically part of the Coptic Orthodox Church, sharing a common theological and liturgical heritage. This connection is reflected in the Ethiopian Orthodox Bible, which includes texts and traditions that are also found in the Coptic tradition. The influence of the Coptic Church is evident in the theological writings, liturgical texts, and ecclesiastical art of the Ethiopian Orthodox Church, contributing to the rich and diverse heritage of the Ethiopian Orthodox Bible.

The cultural and historical context of Ethiopia has also played a crucial role in shaping the Ethiopian Orthodox Bible. Ethiopia's unique geographical location, at the crossroads of Africa, the Middle East, and the

Mediterranean, has made it a melting pot of cultural and religious influences. Over the centuries, Ethiopia has been influenced by various civilizations, including the Egyptians, Greeks, Romans, and Arabs, all of whom have left their mark on Ethiopian culture and religion. This diverse cultural heritage is reflected in the Ethiopian Orthodox Bible, which incorporates elements from various traditions and civilizations, creating a unique and comprehensive spiritual text.

The Ethiopian Orthodox Bible is not just a religious text but a living document that reflects the spiritual, cultural, and historical identity of the Ethiopian people. It is a testament to the enduring faith, resilience, and creativity of the Ethiopian Orthodox Church and its followers. As we trace the roots of the Ethiopian Orthodox Bible, we gain a deeper appreciation for its unique composition, profound themes, and cultural significance. This ancient text continues to inspire and guide the Ethiopian Orthodox faithful, providing a rich and enduring legacy for future generations.

The Ethiopian Orthodox Bible is a timeless treasure, a rich and multifaceted testament to the faith, wisdom, and resilience of the Ethiopian Christian tradition. Its unique composition, profound themes, and deep cultural significance make it a vital and enduring part of the spiritual heritage of Ethiopia and the wider Christian community. As we explore the detailed history and significance of this remarkable text, we gain a deeper appreciation for its role in shaping the faith, identity, and culture of the Ethiopian people, and its enduring relevance for believers around the world.

# Chapter 3

# Unveiling the Apocrypha: History and Significance

The Apocrypha, a collection of ancient texts often regarded with ambiguity in many Christian traditions, holds a place of profound significance within the Ethiopian Orthodox Church. These texts, which include a diverse array of historical narratives, wisdom literature, and apocalyptic visions, provide invaluable insights into the religious and cultural milieu of ancient Judaism and early Christianity. In this chapter, we delve into the definition and historical context of the Apocrypha, explore its role within the Ethiopian Orthodox Church, and uncover its spiritual and theological value that continues to inspire and guide the faithful.

## Definition and Historical Context of the Apocrypha

The term "Apocrypha" originates from the Greek word "apokryphos," meaning "hidden" or "secret." It refers to a collection of ancient Jewish and Christian writings that are not included in the canonical Hebrew Bible but are considered significant in various Christian traditions. These texts, which encompass a wide range of genres including historical accounts, wisdom literature, and apocalyptic visions, were written between 300 BCE and 100 CE, a period marked by significant religious and political upheaval.

The Apocrypha includes books such as Tobit, Judith, the Wisdom of Solomon, Ecclesiasticus (also known as Sirach), Baruch, and the additions to Daniel and Esther, among others. These texts were written in different historical contexts and locations, reflecting the diverse experiences and theological perspectives of Jewish communities during the Second Temple period. The historical backdrop of the Apocrypha includes the Persian period, the Hellenistic era following Alexander the Great's conquests, and the Roman occupation of Judea. Each of these periods brought about significant cultural and religious changes, which are reflected in the themes and narratives of the Apocryphal books.

The Apocrypha was included in the Septuagint, the Greek translation of the Hebrew Bible, which was widely used by Jewish communities in the Hellenistic world and early Christians. However, the status of the Apocrypha varied among different Jewish and Christian groups. While many early Christians accepted these texts as scripture, their canonical status was debated throughout the early centuries of the Christian Church. The development of the Christian biblical canon was a complex process influenced by theological, historical, and cultural factors, leading to differences in the acceptance of the Apocrypha among various Christian traditions.

The Role of the Apocrypha in the Ethiopian Orthodox Church

In the Ethiopian Orthodox Church, the Apocrypha holds a place of honor and reverence, integrated into the broader canon of scripture. Unlike many Western Christian traditions that relegated the Apocrypha to a secondary status or excluded it altogether, the Ethiopian Orthodox Church embraces these texts as integral parts of its spiritual and theological heritage. This inclusion reflects the church's broader understanding of divine revelation and its commitment to preserving a comprehensive and diverse scriptural tradition.

The Ethiopian Orthodox Bible, with its unique composition of 88 books, includes not only the traditional books of the Old and New Testaments but also a significant number of Apocryphal and Pseudepigraphal texts. This expansive canon highlights the Ethiopian Church's inclusive approach to scripture, recognizing the spiritual and theological value of a wide range of writings that contribute to the fullness of divine revelation. The Apocryphal books are used liturgically and devotionally, offering the faithful insights into God's wisdom, guidance in ethical living, and hope in times of trial.

The Book of Tobit, for example, is cherished in the Ethiopian Orthodox tradition for its themes of faith, piety, and divine providence. The story of Tobit's steadfastness in faith and the miraculous healing of his son, Tobias, resonates deeply with the Ethiopian faithful, offering a model of righteous living and trust in God's intervention. Similarly, the Book of Judith, which recounts the courageous actions of a pious widow who delivers her people from oppression, is celebrated for its portrayal of faith, bravery, and divine deliverance.

The Wisdom of Solomon and Ecclesiasticus (Sirach) are valued for their rich theological and ethical teachings. These wisdom texts provide profound insights into the nature of God, the pursuit of righteousness, and the importance of living a virtuous life. Their inclusion in the Ethiopian Orthodox Bible underscores the church's emphasis on wisdom literature as a source of moral and spiritual guidance.

The Apocryphal texts also play a crucial role in the liturgical life of the Ethiopian Orthodox Church. They are read during various liturgical celebrations and feast days, enriching the worship experience with their timeless messages and theological depth. The inclusion of the Apocrypha in the liturgy reflects the Ethiopian Church's commitment to a holistic and inclusive approach to scripture, where all texts that convey divine wisdom and truth are honored and revered.

## The Spiritual and Theological Value of the Apocrypha

The Apocrypha holds profound spiritual and theological value for the Ethiopian Orthodox Church and its followers. These texts offer rich narratives, ethical teachings, and theological reflections that contribute to the church's understanding of God's revelation and the moral and spiritual life of the faithful. The spiritual value of the Apocrypha lies in its ability to inspire, instruct, and guide believers in their journey of faith.

One of the central themes in the Apocrypha is the sovereignty and providence of God. The stories of Tobit, Judith, and the Maccabees, for instance, illustrate God's active involvement in the lives of His people, guiding and delivering them through various trials and tribulations. These narratives reinforce the belief in God's faithfulness and the assurance that He is present and active in the world, working for the good of those who trust in Him.

The Apocryphal texts also provide valuable ethical teachings that are essential for the moral formation of the faithful. The Wisdom of Solomon and Ecclesiasticus (Sirach) offer profound insights into the nature of wisdom, the importance of righteousness, and the virtues of humility, patience, and justice. These teachings are integral to the Ethiopian Orthodox Church's emphasis on ethical living and the pursuit of holiness. The ethical instructions found in the Apocrypha complement the moral teachings of the canonical books, providing a comprehensive framework for living a virtuous and God-centered life.

The theological reflections in the Apocrypha contribute to a deeper understanding of key doctrines and themes in the Ethiopian Orthodox tradition. The Wisdom of Solomon, for example, offers profound insights into the nature of divine wisdom, the immortality of the soul, and the righteous judgment of God. These theological themes resonate with the broader theological framework of the Ethiopian Orthodox Church, enriching its doctrinal teachings and spiritual reflections.

The Apocryphal texts also play a significant role in shaping the liturgical and devotional practices of the Ethiopian Orthodox faithful. The rich narratives, prayers, and hymns found in the Apocrypha are integrated into the liturgical life of the church, enhancing the worship experience with their theological depth and spiritual beauty. The inclusion of the Apocrypha in the liturgy reflects the church's holistic approach to scripture, where all texts that convey divine wisdom and truth are honored and revered.

Moreover, the Apocrypha provides a historical and cultural context that is essential for understanding the development of Jewish and early Christian thought. The historical narratives and theological reflections in the Apocrypha offer valuable insights into the religious and cultural milieu of the Second Temple period, a formative time for both Judaism and Christianity. This historical context enriches the understanding of the canonical scriptures and provides a broader perspective on the development of biblical theology.

The Apocrypha holds a place of profound significance within the Ethiopian Orthodox Church. These ancient texts, with their rich narratives, ethical teachings, and theological reflections, provide invaluable insights into the religious and cultural milieu of ancient Judaism and early Christianity. The inclusion of the Apocrypha in the Ethiopian Orthodox Bible reflects the church's inclusive approach to scripture and its commitment to preserving a comprehensive and diverse spiritual heritage. The spiritual and theological value of the Apocrypha continues to inspire and guide the Ethiopian Orthodox faithful, offering rich narratives, profound ethical teachings, and deep theological reflections that contribute to the church's understanding of God's revelation and the moral and spiritual life of the faithful. As we unveil the Apocrypha, we gain a deeper appreciation for its historical context, its role within the Ethiopian Orthodox Church, and its enduring spiritual and theological significance.

# Chapter 4

# Exploring Apocryphal Books: Tobit and Judith

## Historical and Literary Analysis of Tobit

The Book of Tobit, an essential part of the Apocrypha, offers a rich tapestry of historical, literary, and theological elements that reflect its significance within the Ethiopian Orthodox tradition. Set against the backdrop of the Assyrian Empire, Tobit is a tale of faith, divine intervention, and righteousness that has intrigued scholars and believers for centuries. This book is not just a historical document but a narrative woven with deep moral and theological implications.

Historically, Tobit is set during the Assyrian captivity of the Israelites, a period marked by significant upheaval and exile. The story is framed as a narrative of Tobit, a devout Israelite living in Nineveh, and his trials during this tumultuous time. The text reflects the historical realities of Jewish life under Assyrian rule, including the challenges of maintaining religious identity and integrity amidst foreign oppression. Tobit's unwavering faith and his commitment to Jewish law, even in the face of adversity, underscore the resilience of the Jewish people during this period.

Literarily, the Book of Tobit combines elements of folklore, wisdom literature, and narrative storytelling. The story unfolds with a blend of realism and fantastical elements, such as the journey of Tobit's son, Tobias, who is guided by the archangel Raphael. This blend of the mundane and the miraculous serves to highlight the themes of divine intervention and providence. The narrative structure, with its parallel stories of Tobit's plight and Tobias's journey, creates a rich, interwoven tapestry that emphasizes the book's central themes of faith, healing, and divine justice.

The character development in Tobit is notable for its depth and complexity. Tobit is portrayed as a pious and generous man whose faith is tested through personal suffering and misfortune. His dedication to burying the dead, despite the risks involved, reflects his commitment to Jewish law and the community. Tobias, his son, is depicted as a virtuous young man who undertakes a perilous journey, guided by divine forces, to fulfill his father's request. The interactions between these characters and the resolution of their respective storylines serve to reinforce the book's moral and theological messages.

The book's themes are deeply rooted in Jewish wisdom literature, focusing on the concepts of divine justice, reward for righteousness, and the importance of faithfulness. Tobit's trials and eventual deliverance are portrayed as manifestations of God's justice and mercy. The narrative encourages readers to trust in divine providence, even when faced with seemingly insurmountable challenges. The healing of Tobit's blindness and the successful completion of Tobias's mission are portrayed as direct outcomes of faith and obedience, reinforcing the book's theological message.

In the context of Ethiopian Orthodox tradition, Tobit holds a special place due to its integration into the broader canon of scripture. The book is read and revered for its moral teachings and its portrayal of divine intervention in human affairs. It is often included in liturgical readings and used for reflection during periods of personal or communal crisis. The Ethiopian Orthodox Church's acceptance of Tobit underscores its commitment to preserving a comprehensive scriptural tradition that includes texts with deep theological and moral insights.

The historical and literary analysis of Tobit reveals its significance as both a historical document and a source of spiritual and moral instruction. Its portrayal of divine justice, faithfulness, and righteousness resonates with the broader themes of the Ethiopian Orthodox tradition. The book's rich narrative, combined with its theological messages, makes it a valuable component of the Apocryphal canon and a source of inspiration for believers seeking to understand and live out their faith.

# Historical and Literary Analysis of Judith

The Book of Judith, another key text in the Apocrypha, presents a narrative rich in historical and literary significance. Set during the time of the Babylonian Exile, the story centers on Judith, a widow who becomes an unlikely heroine in the fight against an oppressive foreign power. Judith's story, filled with dramatic events and heroic deeds, offers a unique perspective on themes of faith, courage, and divine intervention.

Historically, Judith is set against the backdrop of the Assyrian Empire's invasion of Israel, specifically during the reign of Nebuchadnezzar. The historical context of the book reflects the political and social tensions of the period, including the struggles of the Jewish people to maintain their identity and sovereignty amidst external threats. The narrative portrays Judith as a courageous woman who takes decisive action to protect her people from impending destruction, reflecting the historical context of resistance against foreign domination.

Literarily, the Book of Judith is characterized by its dramatic and compelling storytelling. The narrative is structured to highlight Judith's heroism and the miraculous nature of her victory over the Assyrian general Holofernes. The story's use of vivid imagery, detailed descriptions, and dramatic tension serves to underscore Judith's role as a divinely inspired deliverer. The contrast between Judith's faith and the arrogance of Holofernes is a central theme, emphasizing the book's moral and theological messages.

Judith's character is portrayed with a mix of strength, intelligence, and piety. Her willingness to take bold and unconventional action to save her people is portrayed as a manifestation of her deep faith and commitment to God. The narrative highlights Judith's strategic acumen and her ability to inspire and lead others in the face of overwhelming odds. Her actions, culminating in the decapitation of Holofernes and the subsequent defeat of the Assyrian army, are presented as acts of divine intervention and justice.

The book's themes of courage, faith, and divine providence are central to its message. Judith's story is a testament to the power of faith and the belief that God can deliver His people from the brink of disaster. The book emphasizes the idea that divine intervention often comes through unexpected means and that true strength and victory come from unwavering faith in God. Judith's triumph serves as a symbol of hope and resilience for the Jewish people and, by extension, for the Ethiopian Orthodox faithful.

In the Ethiopian Orthodox tradition, the Book of Judith is valued for its narrative of faith and deliverance. The book's inclusion in the Ethiopian Orthodox Bible reflects its significance as a source of inspiration and spiritual guidance. Judith's story is often read during times of crisis or challenge, serving as a reminder of God's ability to provide deliverance and protection. The book's themes of faith, courage, and divine intervention resonate deeply with the Ethiopian Orthodox understanding of God's role in the lives of His people.

The historical and literary analysis of Judith reveals its importance as both a historical narrative and a source of spiritual and moral instruction. The book's portrayal of divine intervention, faith, and courage offers valuable insights into the Ethiopian Orthodox tradition's understanding of God's relationship with His people. Judith's story, with its dramatic events and powerful messages, continues to inspire and guide believers in their faith journey.

## Their Roles within Ethiopian Orthodox Tradition

In the Ethiopian Orthodox Church, both the Book of Tobit and the Book of Judith hold significant roles within the broader context of scripture and liturgical practice. Their inclusion in the Ethiopian Orthodox Bible reflects the church's commitment to preserving a comprehensive and diverse scriptural tradition that includes texts with rich theological and moral insights.

The Book of Tobit is often read for its themes of faithfulness, divine intervention, and righteousness. Its narrative of Tobit's suffering, Tobias's journey, and the healing of Tobit's blindness resonates with the Ethiopian Orthodox emphasis on divine providence and the importance of maintaining faith in times of trial. The book is used in liturgical contexts and personal reflection, providing believers with a model of piety and trust in God's plan.

Similarly, the Book of Judith is valued for its dramatic portrayal of faith, courage, and deliverance. Judith's heroic actions and the miraculous defeat of the Assyrian army serve as a powerful reminder of God's ability to provide salvation through unexpected means. The book's themes of courage and divine intervention are integrated into the liturgical life of the Ethiopian Orthodox Church, offering inspiration and encouragement to believers facing their own challenges.

Both books contribute to the Ethiopian Orthodox understanding of scripture and theology by providing diverse perspectives on faith, divine justice, and human resilience. Their inclusion in the Ethiopian Orthodox

Bible reflects the church's inclusive approach to scripture, recognizing the value of a wide range of texts that contribute to a fuller understanding of divine revelation.

The Book of Tobit and the Book of Judith are integral to the Ethiopian Orthodox tradition, offering valuable insights into faith, divine intervention, and moral living. Their historical and literary significance, combined with their roles within the church's liturgical and devotional practices, underscores their importance in the Ethiopian Orthodox Bible and their enduring relevance for the faithful.

# Chapter 5

# Exploring Apocryphal Books: 1 and 2 Maccabees

## Historical Context and Significance of 1 Maccabees

The Book of 1 Maccabees provides a gripping historical account of the Jewish revolt against the Seleucid Empire during the 2nd century BCE, a period of intense religious and political struggle. This book is a key historical document that offers insight into the Maccabean Revolt, a pivotal moment in Jewish history that shaped the identity and religious practices of the Jewish people. The narrative centers on the courageous efforts of the Maccabees, a Jewish family who led a successful rebellion against the oppressive rule of Antiochus IV Epiphanes.

1 Maccabees traces the origins of the revolt to the rise of Antiochus IV, whose harsh policies and desecration of

the Jerusalem Temple prompted widespread unrest among the Jewish population. The book chronicles the initial resistance led by Mattathias, a priest from the Hasmonean family, and his sons, who became the leaders of the revolt. The narrative details their struggles, battles, and eventual victories, culminating in the rededication of the Temple and the establishment of a period of Jewish independence.

Historically, 1 Maccabees is invaluable for its detailed account of the socio-political and religious dynamics of the time. The book provides a vivid portrayal of the challenges faced by the Jewish people under Seleucid rule, including forced Hellenization, religious persecution, and the suppression of Jewish customs. The revolt led by the Maccabees is depicted as a fight for religious freedom and national sovereignty, reflecting the broader struggles of Jewish communities in maintaining their identity and traditions amid foreign domination.

Literarily, 1 Maccabees is characterized by its straightforward, historical narrative style. The book focuses on factual recounting and military achievements, presenting a clear and concise account of the events. Its emphasis on the leadership and valor of the Maccabees highlights the themes of courage, faith, and resistance. The book serves as both a historical record and a source of inspiration for those facing oppression or seeking to uphold their religious beliefs.

In the Ethiopian Orthodox tradition, 1 Maccabees holds a significant place as a testament to the struggles and triumphs of the Jewish people. Its inclusion in the Ethiopian Orthodox Bible underscores the importance of the Maccabean Revolt as a historical and spiritual symbol of resistance against tyranny and oppression. The book's message of perseverance and faith in the face of adversity resonates deeply within the Ethiopian Orthodox community, which values its historical and religious insights.

1 Maccabees also offers a perspective on the importance of religious and national identity. The book's portrayal of the Maccabees' efforts to restore the desecrated Temple

and reinstate Jewish practices highlights the significance of religious freedom and the preservation of cultural heritage. This aspect of the narrative aligns with the Ethiopian Orthodox Church's emphasis on maintaining and defending spiritual and cultural traditions.

## Historical Context and Significance of 2 Maccabees

The Book of 2 Maccabees provides a complementary yet distinct perspective on the Maccabean Revolt, offering a more theological and moral interpretation of the events described in 1 Maccabees. While 1 Maccabees focuses on the historical and military aspects of the revolt, 2 Maccabees emphasizes the religious and spiritual dimensions, highlighting the role of divine intervention and the moral lessons derived from the struggle.

Set in a similar historical context, 2 Maccabees covers the period of the Maccabean Revolt, but it does so with a focus on the martyrdom of the Jewish people and the miraculous events that supported their cause. The book begins with a recounting of the events leading up to the revolt, including the desecration of the Temple and the suffering of Jewish martyrs. It then shifts to a detailed narrative of the revolt, focusing on the actions of Judas Maccabeus and his brothers, who are portrayed as divinely inspired heroes fighting for the preservation of their faith and nation.

Historically, 2 Maccabees provides insight into the religious and spiritual aspects of the Maccabean Revolt. The book highlights the martyrdom of Jewish individuals who refused to abandon their faith, emphasizing their courage and commitment to religious principles. The portrayal of divine intervention and miraculous occurrences in 2 Maccabees serves to underscore the book's theological message that God supports and rewards those who remain faithful in times of trial.

Literarily, 2 Maccabees is characterized by its emphasis on religious themes and moral teachings. The narrative includes speeches, prayers, and reflections on the nature of suffering and divine justice. This literary style contrasts with the more straightforward historical account of 1 Maccabees, offering a deeper exploration of the spiritual and ethical dimensions of the revolt. The book's focus on martyrdom and divine support provides a powerful message of faith and perseverance.

In the Ethiopian Orthodox tradition, 2 Maccabees is valued for its theological insights and spiritual messages. The book's emphasis on divine intervention, martyrdom, and the importance of faith aligns with the Ethiopian Orthodox Church's teachings on the role of God in human affairs and the value of suffering for a righteous cause. The inclusion of 2 Maccabees in the Ethiopian Orthodox Bible reflects the church's commitment to preserving a comprehensive scriptural tradition that includes texts with profound spiritual significance.

The book's role in Ethiopian Orthodox practice includes its use in liturgical readings and personal reflection. The story of the Maccabean martyrs and the miraculous events described in 2 Maccabees serve as sources of inspiration and encouragement for believers facing their own challenges. The book's themes of faith, courage, and divine support resonate with the Ethiopian Orthodox understanding of God's involvement in the lives of His people.

## Their Roles Within Ethiopian Orthodox Tradition

In the Ethiopian Orthodox Church, both 1 and 2 Maccabees are integral to the broader canon of scripture, offering complementary perspectives on the Maccabean Revolt and its significance. Their inclusion in the Ethiopian Orthodox Bible reflects the church's commitment to preserving a diverse and comprehensive scriptural tradition that includes texts with historical, theological, and moral insights.

1 Maccabees is valued for its detailed historical account of the revolt and its portrayal of the Maccabees as heroes of faith and resistance. The book's emphasis on the political and military aspects of the struggle provides a historical context for understanding the challenges faced by the Jewish people under Seleucid rule. Its role in

Ethiopian Orthodox tradition includes serving as a source of inspiration for perseverance and faithfulness in the face of adversity.

2 Maccabees, with its focus on religious themes and divine intervention, complements the historical narrative of 1 Maccabees by providing a deeper exploration of the spiritual and moral dimensions of the revolt. The book's emphasis on martyrdom and divine support offers valuable insights into the Ethiopian Orthodox understanding of faith and the role of God in human affairs. Its role in liturgical practice and personal reflection underscores its significance as a source of spiritual guidance and encouragement.

Together, 1 and 2 Maccabees contribute to the Ethiopian Orthodox tradition by offering diverse perspectives on the Maccabean Revolt and its impact on Jewish identity and faith. Their inclusion in the Ethiopian Orthodox Bible highlights the church's commitment to preserving a rich and varied scriptural heritage that includes texts with deep historical, theological, and moral significance.

The historical context and significance of 1 and 2 Maccabees, along with their roles within the Ethiopian Orthodox tradition, underscore the importance of these texts in understanding the Maccabean Revolt and its impact on religious and cultural identity. The books' contributions to the broader canon of scripture reflect the Ethiopian Orthodox Church's dedication to preserving and honoring a comprehensive and inclusive scriptural tradition.

# Chapter 6

# Exploring Apocryphal Books: Wisdom of Solomon and Ecclesiasticus

## Historical and Literary Analysis of Wisdom of Solomon

The Wisdom of Solomon, also known as the Book of Wisdom, holds a unique place in the Ethiopian Orthodox tradition due to its rich theological content and its poetic appeal. Historically, it is believed to have been written in the late first century BCE, a period marked by Hellenistic influence in the Jewish diaspora, particularly in Alexandria, Egypt. The authorship is traditionally attributed to King Solomon, though modern scholarship suggests it was likely composed by an anonymous Jewish writer well-versed in Greek philosophy and culture.

The text of the Wisdom of Solomon is an intricate blend of Jewish theological thought and Hellenistic philosophy, illustrating a synthesis of Jewish religious tradition with Greco-Roman intellectual culture. It comprises three main sections: the exhortation to seek wisdom, the praise of wisdom, and the role of wisdom in guiding Israel's history. The first section emphasizes the immortality of the soul and the ultimate reward for the righteous. The second section personifies wisdom, depicting it as a divine attribute that guides and sustains the world. The final section recounts the history of Israel through the lens of wisdom's guiding influence, from the Exodus to the Babylonian exile.

The literary style of the Wisdom of Solomon is notable for its eloquent and elevated prose, often resembling the poetic and sapiential texts of the Old Testament. The text employs a variety of literary devices, including parallelism, metaphors, and rhetorical questions, enhancing its didactic and inspirational qualities. The sophisticated Greek language used in the text reflects the educational background of its author, who sought to communicate Jewish wisdom to a Hellenistic audience.

## Historical and Literary Analysis of Ecclesiasticus (Sirach)

Ecclesiasticus, also known as the Wisdom of Sirach or simply Sirach, is another significant apocryphal book within the Ethiopian Orthodox canon. Written by Jesus ben Sirach around 180-175 BCE, it provides a profound insight into Jewish ethical teachings and practical wisdom. The author, a sage from Jerusalem, compiled his work to preserve the Jewish wisdom tradition in the face of growing Hellenistic influences.

The historical context of Ecclesiasticus is crucial to understanding its content and purpose. Composed during the Hellenistic period, Sirach addresses the challenges of maintaining Jewish identity and religious practices amidst the cultural and political pressures of the time. The book is structured as a collection of proverbs, maxims, and ethical teachings, covering a wide range of topics from piety and humility to social justice and proper conduct. Its practical advice is grounded in the Torah and the Jewish wisdom tradition, making it a valuable resource for both religious and everyday life.

Literarily, Ecclesiasticus is characterized by its diverse style, alternating between aphoristic sayings and extended reflections. The use of parallelism, a hallmark of Hebrew poetry, is prominent throughout the text, contributing to its rhythmic and memorable quality. Sirach's teachings are deeply rooted in the Jewish religious and cultural milieu, reflecting a profound reverence for the law, the temple, and the covenant with God. The text also demonstrates a keen observation of human behavior and social dynamics, offering timeless insights into the human condition.

## Their Roles within Ethiopian Orthodox Tradition

In the Ethiopian Orthodox tradition, both the Wisdom of Solomon and Ecclesiasticus hold significant theological and liturgical roles. The inclusion of these books in the Ethiopian Bible underscores the church's comprehensive approach to scripture, embracing both canonical and apocryphal texts to provide a fuller understanding of divine wisdom and moral instruction.

The Wisdom of Solomon is particularly revered for its emphasis on divine wisdom and righteousness. Its teachings on the immortality of the soul and the ultimate vindication of the just resonate deeply within the Ethiopian Orthodox spirituality, which places a strong emphasis on the afterlife and divine justice. The poetic and philosophical nature of the text makes it a rich source for theological reflection and spiritual edification. It is often read and expounded upon during liturgical services and theological discussions, highlighting its enduring relevance in guiding the faithful toward a life of wisdom and righteousness.

Ecclesiasticus, with its practical wisdom and ethical teachings, serves as a moral compass for the Ethiopian Orthodox community. Its comprehensive coverage of ethical and social issues provides a valuable framework for personal conduct and community life. The book's teachings are frequently cited in sermons, catechism, and religious education, offering practical guidance on living a virtuous and pious life. The emphasis on honoring parents, practicing humility, and seeking wisdom aligns closely with the core values of the Ethiopian Orthodox faith, reinforcing the communal and familial aspects of religious life.

Moreover, the Wisdom of Solomon and Ecclesiasticus contribute to the rich liturgical tradition of the Ethiopian Orthodox Church. Their passages are incorporated into various liturgical readings and hymns, enriching the spiritual and devotional experience of the faithful. The poetic and didactic nature of these texts makes them particularly suitable for liturgical use, allowing worshippers to engage with profound theological and ethical insights through prayer and song.

The Wisdom of Solomon and Ecclesiasticus play a vital role within the Ethiopian Orthodox tradition, both as sources of divine wisdom and as guides for ethical living. Their historical and literary richness, combined with their theological depth, ensures their continued relevance and reverence within the Ethiopian Orthodox faith. These apocryphal books not only bridge the gap between Jewish and Hellenistic thought but also provide timeless teachings that resonate with the spiritual and moral aspirations of the Ethiopian Orthodox community.

# Chapter 7

# Exploring Apocryphal Books: Baruch

## Historical and Literary Analysis of Baruch

The Book of Baruch, named after Baruch ben Neriah, the scribe and companion of the prophet Jeremiah, holds a unique place in the corpus of apocryphal literature. Traditionally, Baruch is thought to have been written during the Babylonian exile, around the 6th century BCE. However, modern scholarship often dates its composition to the 2nd century BCE, reflecting a period of significant turmoil and transformation within the Jewish community. The book is addressed to the exiled Jewish community in Babylon, providing both a theological reflection on their suffering and a call to repentance and adherence to the covenant.

Baruch is divided into five distinct sections, each contributing to its overarching themes of repentance, wisdom, and hope. The first section is a historical prologue that sets the context for the book, describing how Baruch read the text in Babylon before King Jehoiachin and the exiled community. This prologue establishes the book's authority and its direct connection to the traumatic experience of exile. The second section consists of a prayer of confession, where the exiles acknowledge their sins and plead for God's mercy. This heartfelt plea highlights the centrality of repentance in restoring the covenant relationship with God.

The third section is a hymn of praise to God, celebrating His wisdom and power. This hymn serves to remind the exiles of God's enduring faithfulness and His ability to restore their fortunes. The fourth section, often referred to as the "Letter of Jeremiah," warns the exiles against idolatry, emphasizing the futility of worshipping false gods. This letter reinforces the importance of exclusive devotion to the God of Israel, even in the face of cultural assimilation and external pressures. The final section of

Baruch is a poem that reflects on the return of wisdom to Israel, symbolizing the hope of restoration and renewal for the Jewish people.

Literarily, Baruch is rich in its use of poetic language, imagery, and rhetorical devices. The prayer of confession employs parallelism and repetition to convey the depth of the community's remorse and their earnest plea for forgiveness. The hymn of praise utilizes vivid descriptions of God's creation and His sovereign power, evoking a sense of awe and reverence. The "Letter of Jeremiah" adopts a didactic tone, using direct address and vivid contrasts to underscore the folly of idolatry. The final poem, with its imagery of light and wisdom, provides a hopeful vision of redemption and enlightenment.

## Its Role within Ethiopian Orthodox Tradition

In the Ethiopian Orthodox tradition, the Book of Baruch holds significant theological and liturgical importance. Its inclusion in the Ethiopian Bible highlights the church's broader canon, which embraces a wide array of texts to offer a comprehensive spiritual and moral framework for the faithful. Baruch's themes of repentance, wisdom, and hope resonate deeply within the Ethiopian Orthodox ethos, where the concepts of sin, redemption, and divine wisdom are central to religious life and practice.

The prayer of confession in Baruch is particularly poignant within the Ethiopian Orthodox context, where communal and individual repentance is a key aspect of spiritual practice. This prayer is often incorporated into liturgical services, especially during periods of fasting and penitence. The heartfelt expressions of remorse and the plea for divine mercy echo the sentiments of the faithful, fostering a sense of humility and contrition. By engaging with Baruch's prayer, worshippers are reminded of their need for God's forgiveness and their commitment to living in accordance with His will.

The hymn of praise in Baruch is also significant in Ethiopian Orthodox worship, where the celebration of

God's wisdom and power is a central theme. This hymn is often recited or sung during liturgical services, enhancing the worship experience with its poetic and exalted language. The depiction of God's creation and His sovereign control over the world serves to inspire awe and reverence among the faithful, reinforcing their trust in God's providence and His ability to guide and protect His people.

The "Letter of Jeremiah" within Baruch serves as a crucial warning against idolatry, a message that has historical and contemporary relevance for the Ethiopian Orthodox Church. Throughout its history, the Ethiopian Church has had to navigate the challenges of external influences and cultural assimilation while maintaining its distinct religious identity. The "Letter of Jeremiah" provides a timeless admonition to remain faithful to the God of Israel, rejecting the allure of false gods and foreign practices. This message is particularly resonant in a modern context, where the church continues to uphold its traditions and teachings amidst the pressures of globalization and modernity.

Furthermore, the final poem in Baruch, with its imagery of wisdom and light, aligns closely with the Ethiopian Orthodox emphasis on divine wisdom and enlightenment. The concept of wisdom as a guiding light for the faithful is a recurring theme in Ethiopian Orthodox theology and spirituality. This poem's vision of wisdom returning to Israel symbolizes the hope of spiritual renewal and restoration, a hope that is central to the Ethiopian Orthodox understanding of salvation and eschatology.

The Book of Baruch plays a vital role within the Ethiopian Orthodox tradition, offering profound theological insights and practical guidance for the faithful. Its themes of repentance, wisdom, and hope are interwoven into the fabric of Ethiopian Orthodox worship and spiritual life, enriching the religious experience and deepening the understanding of God's relationship with His people. Through its prayers, hymns, and admonitions, Baruch continues to inspire and instruct the Ethiopian Orthodox community, affirming their faith and guiding them on their spiritual journey.

# Chapter 8

# The Old Testament: Foundations of Faith

## Overview of the Old Testament Books

The Old Testament, or the Hebrew Bible, is a compilation of texts that forms the foundation of the Ethiopian Orthodox faith, as well as Judaism and Christianity. It is a diverse collection of books that encompass various genres, historical narratives, legal codes, wisdom literature, poetry, and prophecy. In the Ethiopian Orthodox tradition, the Old Testament comprises 46 books, including several that are considered apocryphal in other Christian traditions but are integral to the Ethiopian biblical canon.

The Pentateuch, or the first five books of the Old Testament—Genesis, Exodus, Leviticus, Numbers, and Deuteronomy—lays the groundwork for the narrative of the Israelites, their covenant with God, and the laws that define their relationship with Him. Genesis begins with the creation of the world, the fall of humanity, and the early patriarchs, including Abraham, Isaac, and Jacob. Exodus recounts the liberation of the Israelites from Egyptian bondage and the establishment of the covenant at Mount Sinai. Leviticus, Numbers, and Deuteronomy detail the laws and regulations governing Israelite society, their wilderness journey, and Moses' final speeches before entering the Promised Land.

The historical books—Joshua, Judges, Ruth, 1 and 2 Samuel, 1 and 2 Kings, 1 and 2 Chronicles, Ezra, and Nehemiah—narrate the conquest of Canaan, the establishment of the monarchy, the division of the kingdom, and the eventual exile and return of the Israelites. These books provide a historical framework that traces the highs and lows of the Israelite nation, their fidelity and infidelity to God, and His unwavering commitment to His covenant.

The wisdom literature—Job, Psalms, Proverbs, Ecclesiastes, and the Song of Solomon—offers profound reflections on the human condition, the nature of God, and the pursuit of wisdom. Job explores the problem of suffering and divine justice. Psalms, a collection of lyrical prayers and hymns, express a wide range of emotions, from despair to exuberant praise. Proverbs offers practical advice on living a righteous and wise life. Ecclesiastes contemplates the meaning of life and the futility of worldly pursuits. The Song of Solomon celebrates the beauty of love and human relationships.

The prophetic books, divided into major prophets (Isaiah, Jeremiah, Lamentations, Ezekiel, and Daniel) and minor prophets (Hosea through Malachi), convey messages of warning, hope, and restoration. The prophets call the people back to faithfulness, denounce injustice, and foretell the coming of a messianic age. Their writings are marked by poetic and symbolic language, capturing the urgency and passion of their divine commissions.

In addition to these books, the Ethiopian Orthodox Old Testament includes several deuterocanonical books:

Tobit, Judith, 1 and 2 Maccabees, Wisdom of Solomon, Sirach (Ecclesiasticus), Baruch, and the additions to Esther and Daniel. These books, often excluded from the Protestant canon, provide additional historical narratives, wisdom teachings, and theological insights, enriching the Ethiopian Orthodox understanding of scripture.

## Historical Context, Literary Genres, and Theological Themes

The Old Testament was written over a vast span of time, reflecting the historical, cultural, and theological evolution of the Israelite people. Its historical context encompasses the formation of Israel as a nation, their experiences in Egypt, the Exodus, the conquest of Canaan, the establishment of the monarchy, the division of the kingdom, the Babylonian exile, and the return and restoration period.

Each book of the Old Testament must be understood within its specific historical and cultural milieu. For instance, the Pentateuch reflects ancient Near Eastern law codes and covenantal practices. The historical books align with ancient historiography, emphasizing theological interpretation over mere chronological reporting. Wisdom literature draws from a tradition of sapiential writings common in the ancient Near East, with parallels found in Egyptian and Mesopotamian texts. The prophetic books reflect the socio-political contexts of their times, often addressing contemporary issues such as social justice, religious fidelity, and foreign oppression.

The literary genres within the Old Testament are diverse, each contributing uniquely to its overall message. Narrative genres, found primarily in the Pentateuch and historical books, recount the foundational stories of the Israelite people. Legal codes, embedded within these narratives, outline the covenantal obligations of the Israelites. Wisdom literature employs poetry, aphorisms, and reflective prose to explore profound questions of existence and morality. Prophetic literature uses symbolic language, visions, and oracles to communicate divine messages. The Psalms, a distinct genre of poetic prayer, express a wide range of human emotions in relation to God.

The theological themes of the Old Testament are vast and profound. Central to these themes is the concept of covenant—a binding agreement between God and His people, marked by mutual commitments and responsibilities. This covenantal relationship is established with the patriarchs, reaffirmed at Sinai, and reiterated through the prophets. It underscores God's steadfast love (hesed) and faithfulness, despite the recurring unfaithfulness of His people.

Another major theme is the holiness of God, reflected in His laws and the demand for the Israelites to live set apart (holy) lives. This holiness is manifested in the rituals, sacrifices, and ethical laws detailed in the Pentateuch. The concept of justice is also central, particularly in the prophetic literature, where social justice and righteousness are emphasized as essential aspects of covenant fidelity.

The theme of wisdom, found predominantly in the wisdom literature, explores the fear of the Lord as the beginning of wisdom. This wisdom is not merely intellectual but deeply practical, guiding individuals in righteous living. The Old Testament also grapples with theodicy—the question of divine justice in the face of human suffering—most poignantly in the Book of Job.

Lastly, the theme of messianic hope permeates the prophetic books, with prophecies pointing to a future anointed one (Messiah) who will restore Israel and bring about an era of peace and justice. This hope is a cornerstone of the theological narrative, providing a forward-looking vision that sustains the faith of the Israelite community.

## Unique Features in the Ethiopian Orthodox Old Testament

The Ethiopian Orthodox Old Testament is distinctive in its inclusion of several books not found in the canonical collections of other Christian traditions. These unique features reflect the Ethiopian Church's historical development, its interactions with other Christian and Jewish traditions, and its commitment to preserving a comprehensive scriptural heritage.

One of the most notable unique features is the inclusion of the Book of Enoch, a work of apocalyptic literature that is highly esteemed within the Ethiopian Orthodox tradition. The Book of Enoch, attributed to the antediluvian patriarch Enoch, contains detailed visions of the heavenly realms, the fate of the wicked, and the coming of the Messiah. Its themes of divine judgment, the fallen angels, and the ultimate triumph of righteousness align closely with the eschatological hopes of the Ethiopian Church.

The Ethiopian Orthodox canon also includes Jubilees, a reworking of Genesis and part of Exodus, emphasizing the importance of observing the Sabbath and other sacred times. Jubilees provides a chronological framework for biblical history, divided into periods of jubilees (49 years), and offers detailed expansions on biblical narratives. Its legal and ethical teachings reinforce the covenantal obligations of the Israelites, resonating with the Ethiopian Orthodox emphasis on living in accordance with divine law.

Another unique inclusion is the Book of Baruch and the Letter of Jeremiah, both of which are integral to the Ethiopian Orthodox Old Testament. These texts offer reflections on the Babylonian exile, emphasizing themes of repentance, divine wisdom, and the futility of idolatry. They provide additional context and theological depth to the narrative of Israel's exile and restoration, underscoring the importance of faithfulness to God.

The Ethiopian Orthodox tradition also venerates the Book of 1 Enoch, which contains detailed prophecies and visions, providing a unique apocalyptic perspective on the fate of the world and the coming kingdom of God. This book's inclusion reflects the church's broader acceptance of apocalyptic literature, which offers hope and assurance of God's ultimate justice and triumph.

The presence of these additional books in the Ethiopian Orthodox Old Testament enriches the theological and literary tapestry of the canon, offering a more expansive view of God's dealings with humanity. They highlight the Ethiopian Church's commitment to preserving ancient traditions and texts that provide valuable insights into the history, faith, and practices of the early Jewish and Christian communities.

The Old Testament is the bedrock of the Ethiopian Orthodox faith, encompassing a rich diversity of texts that together narrate the history, laws, wisdom, and prophetic visions of the Israelite people. Its historical context, literary genres, and theological themes provide a comprehensive foundation for understanding the nature of God, the covenantal relationship with His people, and the ethical and spiritual guidelines for living a life of faithfulness and righteousness. The unique features of the Ethiopian Orthodox Old Testament, including its broader canon and distinctive apocryphal books, further enrich this foundation, offering a profound and multifaceted scriptural heritage that continues to inspire and guide the Ethiopian Orthodox faithful.

# Chapter 9

# The New Testament: The Life and Teachings of Christ

## Overview of the New Testament Books

The New Testament is the cornerstone of Christian theology and faith, documenting the life, teachings, death, and resurrection of Jesus Christ, as well as the early years of the Christian church. Comprised of 27 books, the New Testament is a diverse collection that includes the Gospels, historical accounts, epistles, and apocalyptic literature. In the Ethiopian Orthodox tradition, these texts are revered for their divine inspiration and their role in illuminating the path to salvation through Jesus Christ.

The New Testament begins with the four Gospels—Matthew, Mark, Luke, and John. Each Gospel offers a unique perspective on the life and ministry of Jesus. Matthew presents Jesus as the fulfillment of Old

Testament prophecies, emphasizing His role as the Messiah and King. Mark, the shortest and most action-oriented Gospel, portrays Jesus as the suffering servant and Son of God, focusing on His deeds and the immediacy of His mission. Luke, a carefully researched account, highlights Jesus' compassion and outreach to the marginalized, presenting Him as the Savior of all humanity. John, with its profound theological depth, emphasizes the divinity of Christ, portraying Him as the eternal Word made flesh.

Following the Gospels is the Book of Acts, a historical account of the early church's formation and expansion, written by Luke. Acts chronicles the apostles' efforts to spread the Gospel, the challenges they faced, and the transformative work of the Holy Spirit. It serves as a bridge between the Gospels and the Epistles, providing valuable context for understanding the growth and development of early Christian communities.

The Epistles, or letters, constitute the bulk of the New Testament. These writings, primarily authored by the

Apostle Paul, address specific communities and individuals, offering theological insights, ethical instructions, and pastoral guidance. Key Pauline Epistles include Romans, which expounds on justification by faith and the universality of salvation; 1 and 2 Corinthians, which address issues of church unity, morality, and spiritual gifts; Galatians, which defends the Gospel of grace against legalism; and Ephesians, which explores the mystery of the church as the body of Christ.

In addition to Paul's letters, the New Testament includes the General Epistles, written by other apostles and early church leaders. These letters, such as James, 1 and 2 Peter, 1, 2, and 3 John, and Jude, address various doctrinal and practical issues, emphasizing faith, hope, love, and perseverance. The Epistle to the Hebrews stands out for its sophisticated theological argumentation, presenting Jesus as the ultimate high priest and mediator of a new covenant.

The New Testament concludes with the Book of Revelation, an apocalyptic vision attributed to the

Apostle John. Revelation employs vivid imagery and symbolic language to depict the cosmic struggle between good and evil, the ultimate triumph of Christ, and the establishment of a new heaven and earth. It offers hope and encouragement to persecuted Christians, assuring them of God's sovereignty and the certainty of His final victory.

## Historical Context, Literary Genres, and Theological Themes

The New Testament was written in the context of the Roman Empire, a period marked by political stability, cultural diversity, and widespread communication networks. This historical backdrop significantly influenced the spread of Christianity and the development of its early doctrines. The diverse literary genres within the New Testament reflect the multifaceted nature of early Christian witness and teaching.

The Gospels, as a distinct genre, blend elements of biography, history, and theology. They are not mere chronological accounts but carefully crafted narratives that convey the significance of Jesus' life and mission. Each Gospel writer, or evangelist, shapes their account to address the specific needs and concerns of their audience, using parables, discourses, miracles, and passion narratives to reveal the identity and work of Christ.

The Book of Acts, as historical narrative, continues the story of Jesus' followers, emphasizing the role of the Holy Spirit in guiding and empowering the church. Acts employs speeches, travelogues, and dramatic events to illustrate the dynamic and often turbulent expansion of the Christian faith.

The Epistles represent a diverse collection of letters, varying in style and purpose. Pauline Epistles often follow a rhetorical structure, combining theological exposition with practical exhortation. They address both doctrinal issues, such as justification, sanctification, and the nature of the church, and practical concerns, such as ethics, relationships, and community life. The General Epistles, while sharing some of these characteristics, often focus on broader themes of faithfulness, endurance, and the Christian's relationship to the world.

Revelation, as apocalyptic literature, is distinct in its genre and style. It employs symbolic imagery, numerology, and visions to convey its message of hope and judgment. Apocalyptic literature aims to reveal hidden truths about God's plan for history and the ultimate destiny of creation, offering reassurance to believers facing persecution and hardship.

The theological themes of the New Testament are profound and transformative. Central to these themes is the person and work of Jesus Christ. The New Testament presents Jesus as the incarnate Son of God, the promised Messiah, and the Savior of the world. His life, death, and resurrection are the focal point of Christian faith, providing the basis for salvation and the hope of eternal life. The New Testament emphasizes the significance of Jesus' sacrificial death on the cross, His victorious resurrection, and His exaltation as Lord and King.

Another major theme is the kingdom of God. Jesus' teachings and parables often center on the kingdom, depicting it as both a present reality and a future hope. The kingdom of God represents God's sovereign rule, characterized by justice, peace, and righteousness. Believers are called to live as citizens of this kingdom, embodying its values and proclaiming its message.

The theme of salvation is intricately woven throughout the New Testament. Salvation is presented as a gift of God's grace, received through faith in Jesus Christ. It encompasses forgiveness of sins, reconciliation with God, and transformation by the Holy Spirit. The New Testament also emphasizes the communal aspect of salvation, highlighting the church as the body of Christ and the family of believers.

The New Testament addresses the role of the Holy Spirit in the life of the believer and the church. The Spirit is depicted as the divine agent of regeneration, empowerment, and guidance. The Spirit's work is essential for understanding Scripture, living a holy life, and fulfilling the mission of the church.

Ethical and moral teachings are also prominent in the New Testament. Jesus' Sermon on the Mount, Paul's ethical instructions, and the practical exhortations in the General Epistles provide a comprehensive guide for Christian living. These teachings emphasize love, humility, service, and holiness, calling believers to reflect the character of Christ in their daily lives.

## Unique Features in the Ethiopian Orthodox New Testament

The Ethiopian Orthodox New Testament is notable for its inclusion of additional books and unique features that distinguish it from other Christian traditions. One of the most significant differences is the inclusion of the Book of Enoch and the Book of Jubilees, which are considered canonical in the Ethiopian Orthodox Church but are not part of the New Testament in other traditions. These books provide additional insights into the theological and historical context of early Christianity and the beliefs of the Ethiopian Orthodox community.

The Ethiopian Orthodox New Testament also includes several other texts that are considered apocryphal or deuterocanonical in other traditions. These include the Prayer of Manasseh, 3 Maccabees, and Psalm 151. The inclusion of these texts reflects the Ethiopian Church's broader canon and its commitment to preserving a comprehensive scriptural heritage.

The Book of Enoch, in particular, holds a special place in the Ethiopian Orthodox tradition. Attributed to the antediluvian patriarch Enoch, this book contains detailed visions and prophecies, exploring themes of divine judgment, the fallen angels, and the ultimate triumph of righteousness. Its apocalyptic and eschatological themes align closely with the Ethiopian Church's theological emphasis on the final judgment and the hope of eternal life.

The Book of Jubilees, also known as the "Little Genesis," is another unique inclusion in the Ethiopian Orthodox New Testament. This book offers a reworked account of the biblical narratives from Genesis and part of Exodus, emphasizing the importance of observing the Sabbath and other sacred times. Jubilees provides a chronological framework for biblical history, divided into periods of jubilees (49 years), and offers detailed expansions on biblical stories, reinforcing the covenantal obligations of the Israelites.

The inclusion of these additional texts enriches the theological and literary tapestry of the Ethiopian Orthodox New Testament, offering a more expansive view of God's dealings with humanity. They highlight the Ethiopian Church's commitment to preserving ancient traditions and texts that provide valuable insights into the history, faith, and practices of early Jewish and Christian communities.

Another unique feature of the Ethiopian Orthodox New Testament is its distinctive liturgical and devotional use.

The Ethiopian Church has a rich tradition of liturgical worship, and the New Testament is central to its daily prayers, hymns, and sacramental practices. The Gospels are read during the Divine Liturgy, and the Epistles are recited in various liturgical services. The New Testament's teachings and stories are deeply embedded in the Ethiopian Orthodox liturgical calendar and devotional life, shaping the spiritual formation of the faithful.

The Ethiopian Orthodox New Testament also reflects the church's unique theological and cultural context. The Ethiopian Church has a long history of interaction with Jewish and Christian traditions, and this is reflected in its scriptural canon and theological emphases. The themes of covenant, divine judgment, and eschatological hope are particularly prominent, resonating with the Ethiopian Church's historical experiences of persecution, resilience, and renewal.

The New Testament is the heart of the Ethiopian Orthodox faith, encompassing a rich diversity of texts that together narrate the life, teachings, death, and resurrection of Jesus Christ, as well as the early years of the Christian church. Its historical context, literary genres, and theological themes provide a comprehensive foundation for understanding the nature of Christ, the kingdom of God, and the transformative power of salvation. The unique features of the Ethiopian Orthodox New Testament, including its broader canon and distinctive apocryphal books, further enrich this foundation, offering a profound and multifaceted scriptural heritage that continues to inspire and guide the Ethiopian Orthodox faithful. The New Testament's central message of God's love, grace, and redemption through Jesus Christ remains a beacon of hope and a source of strength for believers, inviting them to live out their faith with courage, compassion, and conviction.

# Chapter 10

# The Pseudepigrapha: Expanding the Canon

## Introduction to the Pseudepigrapha

The term "Pseudepigrapha" refers to a diverse collection of ancient writings attributed to biblical figures, yet not included in the canonical scriptures of most Jewish and Christian traditions. These texts, ranging from apocalyptic visions to ethical teachings, offer profound insights into the religious and cultural milieu of the Second Temple period. They reflect the complex and dynamic nature of Jewish thought and the evolving theological landscape that would profoundly influence early Christianity. For the Ethiopian Orthodox Church, certain Pseudepigraphal texts hold a place of reverence and are integrated into their broader scriptural canon, providing a unique perspective on biblical history and theology.

The Pseudepigrapha encompasses a wide array of genres, including apocalypses, testaments, expansions of biblical narratives, and wisdom literature. These texts were often composed between the third century BCE and the second century CE, a time of significant upheaval and transformation in Jewish history. The Pseudepigrapha was produced in response to the social, political, and religious challenges faced by Jewish communities during this period. They reflect a deep engagement with the Hebrew Scriptures, often reinterpreting and expanding upon traditional narratives to address contemporary concerns.

The Pseudepigrapha's attribution to renowned biblical figures such as Enoch, Abraham, Moses, and others, aimed to lend these texts authority and credibility. These attributions were not intended to deceive but rather to honor the legacy of these figures and to assert continuity with the ancient traditions they represented. The Pseudepigrapha served as a means for later generations to explore and articulate their faith, drawing on the wisdom and experiences of their revered ancestors.

# Historical and Literary Analysis of Key Books

The Pseudepigrapha includes numerous texts, but among the most influential are 1 Enoch and Jubilees. These works offer valuable insights into the religious thought and literary creativity of their time, revealing the rich tapestry of beliefs and practices that shaped early Judaism and Christianity.

## 1 Enoch

The Book of Enoch, also known as 1 Enoch, is a compilation of five distinct sections: the Book of the Watchers, the Book of Parables, the Astronomical Book, the Book of Dream Visions, and the Epistle of Enoch. Each section offers unique perspectives on divine judgment, cosmic order, and eschatological hope. 1 Enoch was highly regarded in various Jewish and early Christian communities, influencing theological concepts and scriptural interpretations.

The Book of the Watchers, the oldest section of 1 Enoch, provides a detailed account of the fall of the Watchers, a group of angels who descended to earth and transgressed divine boundaries by taking human wives and teaching forbidden knowledge. This narrative explores themes of corruption, divine retribution, and the ultimate restoration of justice. The Watchers' descent and subsequent punishment highlight the consequences of disobedience and the inevitability of divine judgment.

The Book of Parables, also known as the Similitudes of Enoch, offers visions of the coming judgment and the vindication of the righteous. This section introduces the figure of the "Son of Man," a messianic redeemer who will bring justice and establish God's kingdom. The Son of Man's role as a mediator and judge reflects the hope for divine intervention and the establishment of a righteous order.

The Astronomical Book, or the Book of the Heavenly Luminaries, provides a detailed account of celestial phenomena and their significance. It emphasizes the ordered nature of the cosmos, governed by divine laws and principles. This section underscores the importance of observing heavenly signs and maintaining cosmic harmony, reflecting a worldview that integrates natural and supernatural realms.

The Book of Dream Visions, or the Animal Apocalypse, presents a symbolic history of Israel from the creation to the eschatological future. Using vivid animal imagery, this section recounts the rise and fall of nations, the suffering of the righteous, and the ultimate triumph of God's people. The Animal Apocalypse offers a visionary interpretation of history, emphasizing divine providence and the hope for redemption.

The Epistle of Enoch, the final section of 1 Enoch, addresses ethical and theological concerns, exhorting readers to live righteously and anticipate the coming judgment. It reinforces the themes of divine justice, the fate of the wicked, and the reward of the faithful. The Epistle of Enoch serves as a call to steadfastness and faithfulness in the face of adversity.

1 Enoch's influence extends beyond Jewish traditions, impacting early Christian thought and apocalyptic literature. The themes of angelic rebellion, divine judgment, and messianic hope resonate in the New Testament, particularly in the Gospels, the Pauline Epistles, and the Book of Revelation. Early church fathers, such as Tertullian and Origen, acknowledged 1 Enoch's significance, although its canonical status varied among Christian communities.

## Jubilees

The Book of Jubilees, also known as the "Little Genesis," is a retelling of the Genesis and part of the Exodus narratives, structured around a series of jubilees, or 49-year periods. Jubilees emphasizes the importance of the Sabbath, covenantal fidelity, and the distinctiveness of Israel as God's chosen people. It reflects a deep concern for maintaining religious and cultural identity amidst external influences and internal challenges.

Jubilees begins with a celestial revelation given to Moses on Mount Sinai, where he receives the history of the world from creation to the Exodus, divided into jubilees. This heavenly origin underscores the text's authority and its continuity with Mosaic tradition. The narrative structure, anchored in the concept of jubilees, provides a chronological framework that highlights the cyclical nature of sacred history.

One of the central themes of Jubilees is the sanctity of the Sabbath. The text underscores the significance of the seventh day as a perpetual sign of the covenant between God and Israel. It provides detailed instructions on Sabbath observance and condemns any deviation from its strict observance. The emphasis on the Sabbath reflects a broader concern for maintaining ritual purity and adherence to divine commandments.

Jubilees also addresses the importance of covenantal fidelity, urging the Israelites to remain faithful to God's laws and commandments. It expands on the covenantal themes found in Genesis, emphasizing the special status of Israel as God's chosen people. The text recounts the patriarchal narratives with additional details and interpretations that reinforce the importance of covenantal loyalty and obedience.

Another key aspect of Jubilees is its focus on genealogies and the transmission of sacred traditions. The text provides detailed genealogical lists and elaborates on the lives of the patriarchs, offering moral and ethical lessons derived from their experiences. This emphasis on lineage and heritage underscores the continuity of God's promises and the transmission of divine knowledge across generations.

Jubilees also reflects a heightened awareness of the cosmic struggle between good and evil. It expands on the narrative of the Watchers from 1 Enoch, detailing their descent, transgressions, and punishment. This cosmic conflict is woven into the fabric of sacred history, illustrating the ongoing battle between the forces of righteousness and wickedness.

Jubilees' influence is evident in various Jewish and Christian writings. Its themes and interpretations resonate in the Dead Sea Scrolls, particularly the sectarian writings of the Qumran community, which shared a similar emphasis on covenantal fidelity and eschatological hope. Early Christian texts, including the New Testament, also reflect the influence of Jubilees, particularly in their use of genealogies, eschatological imagery, and ethical exhortations.

## Their Influence on Ancient Judaism and Christianity

The Pseudepigrapha, including 1 Enoch and Jubilees, played a significant role in shaping the religious and theological landscape of ancient Judaism and early Christianity. These texts provided a rich reservoir of ideas, symbols, and narratives that informed the beliefs and practices of various communities.

In ancient Judaism, the Pseudepigrapha contributed to the development of key theological concepts, such as angelology, demonology, and eschatology. The detailed accounts of angelic hierarchies, the fall of the Watchers, and the cosmic struggle between good and evil influenced Jewish thought and practice. These themes are evident in the Dead Sea Scrolls, the writings of Philo and Josephus, and later rabbinic literature.

The Pseudepigrapha also shaped Jewish apocalypticism, a worldview that anticipated divine intervention in history to bring about the ultimate vindication of the righteous and the establishment of God's kingdom. The apocalyptic visions and prophecies in texts like 1 Enoch and Jubilees provided hope and encouragement to Jewish communities facing persecution and hardship. They articulated a theology of divine justice and cosmic order that affirmed God's sovereignty and the certainty of eschatological fulfillment.

In early Christianity, the Pseudepigrapha influenced the development of Christology, soteriology, and eschatology. The figure of the Son of Man in 1 Enoch, for example, provided a messianic framework that early Christians applied to Jesus, interpreting His life, death, and resurrection as the fulfillment of apocalyptic prophecies. The themes of divine judgment, the resurrection of the dead, and the establishment of a new creation resonated with early Christian beliefs and were incorporated into the New Testament writings.

The Pseudepigrapha also contributed to early Christian ethical teachings. The emphasis on righteousness, covenantal fidelity, and the pursuit of holiness found in texts like Jubilees aligned with the moral exhortations of the New Testament. The Pseudepigrapha's portrayal of exemplary figures, such as Enoch, Abraham, and Moses, provided models of faith and obedience for early Christian communities.

The Pseudepigrapha's impact extended to early Christian liturgy and devotional practices. Texts like 1 Enoch and Jubilees were read and revered in certain Christian circles, particularly among those who valued their apocalyptic and ethical teachings. The incorporation of Pseudepigraphal motifs and themes into Christian hymns, prayers, and homilies enriched the spiritual life of early believers.

The Pseudepigrapha represents a vital and dynamic aspect of the ancient Jewish and early Christian literary tradition. These texts, with their diverse genres and profound theological insights, expanded the canon of sacred literature and offered a rich tapestry of religious thought and practice. For the Ethiopian Orthodox Church, the inclusion of certain Pseudepigraphal texts in their broader scriptural canon reflects a deep appreciation for the spiritual and theological heritage of these writings.

The historical and literary analysis of key Pseudepigraphal books, such as 1 Enoch and Jubilees, reveals their enduring significance and influence. These texts provided ancient communities with a framework for understanding divine justice, cosmic order, and eschatological hope. They articulated a vision of faith that affirmed God's sovereignty, the righteousness of the faithful, and the ultimate triumph of good over evil.

The Pseudepigrapha's impact on ancient Judaism and early Christianity is evident in their theological developments, ethical teachings, and devotional practices. These texts enriched the religious imagination of believers, offering a source of inspiration, guidance, and hope. The enduring legacy of the Pseudepigrapha continues to resonate in contemporary religious thought, reflecting the timeless quest for understanding and experiencing the divine.

# Chapter 11

# Influence on Ethiopian Society

## The Bible's Role in Shaping Ethiopian Social Structures

The Bible has been a cornerstone in shaping Ethiopian society for centuries, intertwining with its cultural, social, and political fabric. The Ethiopian Orthodox Tewahedo Church, one of the oldest Christian traditions in the world, has played a pivotal role in disseminating biblical teachings and integrating them into the core of Ethiopian life. The Bible's profound influence is evident in the nation's social structures, laws, customs, and daily practices, reflecting a deep and abiding reverence for its sacred texts.

Ethiopia's embrace of Christianity dates back to the fourth century when King Ezana of Aksum converted to the faith. This monumental event marked the beginning of the Ethiopian Orthodox Church's profound impact on the nation's identity. The Bible, particularly the Ethiopian Orthodox canon, which includes a broader range of texts than other Christian traditions, became the spiritual and moral compass for the Ethiopian people. Its teachings permeated every aspect of society, from governance and legal systems to education and family life.

The hierarchical structure of the Ethiopian Orthodox Church mirrors the organizational framework of the nation. At the apex is the Patriarch, followed by archbishops, bishops, and priests who serve as spiritual leaders and moral guides. This ecclesiastical hierarchy has historically intertwined with the political authority, influencing decisions and policies that align with biblical principles. The symbiotic relationship between church and state has ensured that the Bible's teachings are deeply embedded in the governance and societal norms of Ethiopia.

The church's role extends beyond spiritual guidance; it has been a crucial institution in education and social welfare. Monasteries and churches have historically been centers of learning, preserving ancient manuscripts and imparting biblical knowledge to successive generations. The Bible's teachings on charity, compassion, and justice have driven the church's involvement in social services, providing aid to the needy, supporting orphanages, and advocating for the marginalized.

## Influence on Laws, Customs, and Daily Life

The Bible's influence on Ethiopian laws is profound and enduring. Many of the nation's legal principles are derived from biblical precepts, reflecting a commitment to justice, equity, and moral integrity. The Fetha Nagast, or "Law of the Kings," is a significant legal code that has guided Ethiopian jurisprudence for centuries. Compiled in the 13th century, it incorporates biblical laws and Christian ethical teachings, forming the foundation of Ethiopia's legal system. The Fetha Nagast addresses various aspects of civil and criminal law, governance, and personal conduct, emphasizing the importance of righteousness and moral accountability.

One of the key areas where biblical influence is evident is in family and marital laws. The sanctity of marriage, as emphasized in the Bible, is upheld through legal provisions that promote fidelity, mutual respect, and the protection of family integrity. Divorce is discouraged, and efforts are made to resolve marital disputes in accordance with biblical teachings on reconciliation and forgiveness. The biblical model of family, with its emphasis on love, respect, and duty, is reflected in societal expectations and legal frameworks.

Customs and traditions in Ethiopia are deeply rooted in biblical teachings. Religious festivals, such as Timkat (Epiphany) and Fasika (Easter), are celebrated with great fervor, reflecting the biblical narratives of Christ's baptism and resurrection. These festivals are not merely religious observances but are integral to the cultural identity of the Ethiopian people. They foster a sense of community, continuity, and shared faith, reinforcing the nation's Christian heritage.

Daily life in Ethiopia is imbued with biblical values and practices. The rhythm of life is punctuated by prayer, worship, and adherence to religious rituals. The Ethiopian Orthodox faithful observe regular fasting periods, such as the Lenten fast, which lasts for 55 days. Fasting is not merely an act of abstention but a spiritual discipline that fosters self-control, humility, and a deeper connection with God. The biblical injunctions on fasting and prayer are taken to heart, influencing dietary habits and daily schedules.

The Bible's teachings on hospitality and generosity are also reflected in Ethiopian customs. Visitors are warmly welcomed and offered food and drink, reflecting the biblical principle of treating strangers with kindness and respect. This tradition of hospitality is deeply ingrained in Ethiopian culture, fostering social cohesion and mutual support. The practice of sharing meals, particularly during religious festivals, underscores the importance of community and the biblical ideal of living in harmony with one another.

Education in Ethiopia has historically been influenced by biblical teachings. Church schools and monasteries have been centers of learning, imparting not only religious knowledge but also literacy, history, and the arts. The Bible has been a primary text for instruction, shaping the moral and intellectual development of students. The emphasis on wisdom, knowledge, and the fear of the Lord, as extolled in the biblical books of Proverbs and Ecclesiastes, underscores the value placed on education and moral integrity.

The Bible's influence extends to Ethiopian art, music, and literature. The rich tradition of Ethiopian iconography, with its vivid depictions of biblical scenes and saints, reflects a deep reverence for the sacred texts. Religious music, including the unique liturgical chants of the Ethiopian Orthodox Church, draws inspiration from the Psalms and other biblical hymns. Ethiopian literature, both ancient and contemporary, often weaves biblical themes and moral teachings into its narratives, reflecting the profound impact of the Bible on the nation's cultural expression.

The Bible's teachings on justice, mercy, and compassion have also influenced Ethiopia's approach to social issues. The church's involvement in social justice initiatives, advocacy for the poor, and support for peace and reconciliation efforts are grounded in biblical principles. The prophetic call to "act justly, love mercy, and walk humbly with your God" (Micah 6:8) resonates in the church's mission to address social injustices and promote the common good.

In the realm of governance, Ethiopian leaders have historically drawn on biblical wisdom to guide their decisions. The principles of servant leadership, as exemplified by Christ, have inspired a model of governance that emphasizes humility, integrity, and a commitment to the welfare of the people. The biblical narrative of King Solomon, renowned for his wisdom and just rule, serves as an ideal for Ethiopian rulers, emphasizing the importance of seeking divine guidance in governance.

The Bible's impact on Ethiopian society is also evident in its approach to conflict resolution and peacebuilding. The biblical teachings on forgiveness, reconciliation, and love for one's enemies have guided efforts to resolve conflicts and build lasting peace. The church's role in mediating disputes and fostering dialogue reflects the biblical mandate to be peacemakers and agents of reconciliation.

The enduring influence of the Bible on Ethiopian society is a testament to the deep and abiding faith of the Ethiopian people. The sacred texts have not only shaped the nation's religious identity but have also provided a moral and ethical framework that continues to guide social conduct, governance, and cultural expression. The Bible's teachings on justice, compassion, and righteousness remain a source of inspiration and strength, offering a timeless vision of a society rooted in faith and guided by divine principles.

As Ethiopia continues to navigate the challenges of the modern world, the Bible's influence remains a steadfast anchor, providing a moral compass and a source of hope. The integration of biblical values into the fabric of Ethiopian society underscores the enduring relevance of the sacred texts and their capacity to inspire, transform, and sustain a vibrant and resilient nation.

The Bible's role in shaping Ethiopian social structures, laws, customs, and daily life is profound and far-reaching. The sacred texts have provided a moral and ethical foundation that has guided the nation's development and identity for centuries. The Ethiopian Orthodox Church's commitment to preserving and disseminating biblical teachings has ensured that the Bible's influence remains a vital and enduring force in Ethiopian society. The integration of biblical principles into the nation's social and cultural fabric reflects a deep and abiding reverence for the sacred texts, offering a timeless vision of a society rooted in faith and guided by divine principles.

# Chapter 12

# Art, Music, and Identity

## The Impact of the Bible on Ethiopian Art

Ethiopian art, renowned for its vibrant colors and distinctive iconography, has been profoundly shaped by the Bible. From the earliest Christian frescoes to contemporary expressions, biblical themes and narratives have been central to Ethiopian artistic traditions. The Ethiopian Orthodox Church, with its rich heritage and deep reverence for the Bible, has played a crucial role in the development and preservation of this unique artistic style.

The tradition of Ethiopian Christian art began in the Aksumite period (circa 4th-7th centuries) and was significantly influenced by the introduction of Christianity to the region. Early Ethiopian art often depicted biblical scenes and figures in a style that combined local artistic traditions with Christian iconography. The influence of the Bible is evident in the depiction of key biblical figures such as Christ, the Virgin Mary, and the saints, as well as in scenes from both the Old and New Testaments. These artworks served not only as devotional objects but also as tools for teaching and reinforcing biblical stories to the faithful.

One of the most distinctive features of Ethiopian art is its use of iconography. Ethiopian icons are characterized by their bold colors, stylized figures, and symbolic representations. Biblical stories are depicted with a sense of timelessness and spiritual significance, emphasizing the eternal nature of the divine. The icons often feature geometric patterns and symbolic elements that reflect theological concepts and spiritual truths. For example, the depiction of Christ Pantocrator (Christ as the Almighty) in Ethiopian art is a powerful symbol of Christ's divine authority and presence.

Ethiopian murals, often found in churches and monasteries, offer another rich dimension of biblical influence on art. These murals depict a wide range of biblical scenes, from the Annunciation and the Nativity to the Crucifixion and Resurrection. The murals are not merely decorative but are intended to convey theological messages and reinforce the religious teachings of the Church. They create a visual narrative that guides the viewer through the sacred history of salvation, making the biblical stories accessible and relatable to the congregation.

The Bible's impact on Ethiopian art extends to illuminated manuscripts as well. Ethiopian Gospel books, known as "Mäṣḥāf," are renowned for their elaborate illustrations and decorative elements. These manuscripts often feature detailed illuminations of biblical scenes, saints, and angels, accompanied by ornate borders and calligraphy. The artistry of these manuscripts reflects the high value placed on the written Word of God and the desire to honor it through beauty and craftsmanship.

Ethiopian art has also embraced the biblical themes of redemption and salvation in its portrayal of martyrdom and saints. The depiction of saints and martyrs in Ethiopian art serves as a testament to their spiritual significance and their role as intercessors for the faithful. These artworks often include detailed accounts of the saints' lives and miracles, providing inspiration and guidance to the believers.

The Bible's influence on Ethiopian art is also evident in the use of religious symbols. For instance, the Ethiopian cross, with its unique shape and design, is a prominent symbol in Ethiopian Christian art. It represents the centrality of the crucifixion and resurrection of Christ, which are pivotal events in Christian theology. The cross is often adorned with intricate patterns and motifs that reflect the rich artistic heritage of Ethiopia.

In modern times, the impact of the Bible on Ethiopian art continues to be significant. Contemporary artists draw on traditional biblical themes and styles while incorporating new techniques and perspectives. This blending of the old and the new reflects the ongoing relevance of biblical narratives and their ability to inspire creativity and innovation in the arts.

Overall, the Bible has left an indelible mark on Ethiopian art, shaping its forms, styles, and themes. The artistic expressions of Ethiopian Christianity are a testament to the profound influence of the Bible and its role in enriching the cultural and spiritual life of the Ethiopian people.

## Influence on Traditional and Contemporary Ethiopian Music

The Bible's influence on Ethiopian music is profound and multifaceted, impacting both traditional and contemporary musical practices. Ethiopian Christian music, deeply rooted in the liturgical traditions of the Ethiopian Orthodox Church, reflects the rich heritage and spiritual depth of the biblical narrative.

Traditional Ethiopian liturgical music, known for its unique modes and rhythms, is an integral part of religious worship. The music is characterized by its use of ancient hymns, chants, and melodies that have been passed down through generations. Biblical texts are central to these musical traditions, with hymns and chants often based on scripture and theological themes. The music serves as both a form of worship and a means of meditating on the divine mysteries.

The Ethiopian Orthodox Church's use of the "Zema" or "musical system" is a key feature of its liturgical music. The Zema includes various modes and scales that are used to convey different emotional and spiritual qualities. Biblical psalms and other scriptural texts are sung in these modes, creating a musical expression that enhances the liturgical experience and draws the worshippers into a deeper spiritual connection with the sacred texts.

One of the most distinctive forms of Ethiopian liturgical music is the "Ge'ez chant," which is performed in the ancient Ge'ez language, the liturgical language of the Ethiopian Orthodox Church. The Ge'ez chant is characterized by its melismatic style, where a single syllable is sung over multiple notes. This style of singing allows for an expressive and reverent rendering of biblical texts, creating a powerful and immersive worship experience.

In addition to its liturgical role, biblical themes also permeate Ethiopian folk music and traditional songs. Folk songs often incorporate biblical stories and moral teachings, reflecting the integration of religious values into daily life. These songs are performed at various social and cultural events, including festivals, weddings, and communal gatherings, serving as a way to reinforce and celebrate the biblical heritage of the Ethiopian people.

Contemporary Ethiopian music has also been influenced by the Bible, though it often blends traditional elements with modern genres. Gospel music, in particular, has gained popularity in Ethiopia, reflecting the growing influence of contemporary Christian worship practices. Ethiopian gospel artists draw on biblical themes and narratives, using modern musical styles to express their faith and connect with a broader audience.

The fusion of traditional and contemporary musical elements in Ethiopian gospel music illustrates the dynamic nature of biblical influence in modern contexts. Artists incorporate traditional melodies and rhythms while embracing new musical trends, creating a genre that resonates with both the spiritual and cultural aspects of Ethiopian identity.

The Bible's impact on Ethiopian music is not limited to religious contexts; it also extends to national and cultural expressions. Music festivals, cultural events, and public celebrations often feature performances that reflect biblical themes and narratives. These events provide an opportunity for Ethiopians to celebrate their religious heritage and cultural identity through music.

Overall, the Bible's influence on Ethiopian music is a testament to its deep and enduring impact on the spiritual and cultural life of the nation. From traditional liturgical chants to contemporary gospel songs, biblical themes and narratives continue to inspire and shape the musical expressions of the Ethiopian people.

## The Bible's Role in Forging Ethiopian Identity

The Bible has played a central role in forging Ethiopian identity, shaping the nation's cultural, social, and spiritual fabric. The deep integration of biblical teachings into Ethiopian society has contributed to a distinct national identity that is closely linked to the nation's Christian heritage.

Ethiopia's long history of Christianity, dating back to the fourth century, has profoundly influenced the nation's identity. The Bible, as the sacred text of Ethiopian Orthodox Christianity, has been a foundational element in shaping the nation's values, traditions, and worldview. The Christian faith has been a unifying force, providing a shared sense of purpose and belonging among the Ethiopian people.

The Ethiopian Orthodox Church, with its rich biblical traditions, has been a key institution in shaping national identity. The Church's influence extends beyond religious practices to include social, cultural, and political aspects of Ethiopian life. The Bible's teachings on justice, compassion, and community have guided the Church's mission and shaped its role in society.

Biblical narratives and themes are deeply embedded in Ethiopian cultural expressions, including art, music, and literature. The depiction of biblical stories and figures in Ethiopian art and the use of biblical themes in traditional and contemporary music reflect the integration of biblical values into cultural identity. These artistic expressions serve as a means of celebrating and reinforcing the nation's Christian heritage.

The Bible has also influenced Ethiopian social customs and traditions. Religious festivals, such as Timkat (Epiphany) and Fasika (Easter), are celebrated with great enthusiasm and are integral to the nation's cultural identity. These festivals not only commemorate key biblical events but also serve as occasions for communal gathering and expression of faith.

The Bible's role in forging Ethiopian identity is also evident in the nation's legal and social structures. The integration of biblical principles into the legal system, family laws, and social customs reflects the deep connection between faith and daily life. The emphasis on justice, morality, and community cohesion, as derived from biblical teachings, has shaped the nation's values and social norms.

Ethiopian identity is also shaped by the nation's unique biblical heritage. The Ethiopian Orthodox Church's broader canon, including texts that are not found in other Christian traditions, contributes to a distinctive theological and cultural identity. The preservation and reverence of these texts reflect a commitment to maintaining a unique and authentic expression of Christianity.

The Bible's influence on Ethiopian identity is also reflected in the nation's approach to education and intellectual life. The Church's role in preserving and transmitting biblical knowledge through monasteries and schools has contributed to a strong intellectual tradition. The emphasis on wisdom, learning, and moral integrity, as reflected in biblical teachings, continues to guide educational practices and intellectual pursuits.

In modern times, the Bible's role in forging Ethiopian identity remains significant. The nation's Christian heritage continues to shape its cultural, social, and political landscape, providing a source of inspiration and guidance in navigating contemporary challenges. The integration of biblical values into modern life reflects the enduring relevance of the Bible in shaping Ethiopian identity.

Overall, the Bible's role in forging Ethiopian identity is a testament to its profound and lasting impact on the nation's cultural, social, and spiritual life. The integration of biblical teachings into various aspects of Ethiopian life underscores the deep connection between faith and identity, shaping the nation's values, traditions, and sense of belonging.

# Chapter 13

# Historical Disputes Over Canonicity

## Historical Debates Within the Church

The Ethiopian Orthodox Church's history is marked by complex and profound debates over the canonicity of biblical texts. These disputes reflect broader theological, cultural, and historical tensions within Christianity. The process of determining which books were considered canonical involved intense deliberations among church leaders and scholars, influenced by a variety of theological, historical, and ecclesiastical factors.

The Ethiopian Orthodox canon, renowned for its inclusion of additional texts not found in other Christian traditions, has been a focal point of debate. This canon includes books such as Enoch, Jubilees, and various other apocryphal and pseudepigraphal writings. These texts, while accepted in Ethiopian tradition, have been contested by other Christian denominations that adhere to a more narrowly defined canon. The inclusion of these texts reflects a unique aspect of Ethiopian Orthodox theology and tradition, which emphasizes the diversity and richness of the biblical witness.

One significant historical dispute within the Ethiopian Orthodox Church concerned the status of the Book of Enoch. This ancient text, with its elaborate descriptions of angels and apocalyptic visions, was accepted by Ethiopian Christians but was excluded from the canon of most other Christian traditions. The debates over Enoch's canonicity involved discussions on its theological content, historical origins, and its place within the broader Christian scriptural tradition.

Similarly, the Book of Jubilees faced scrutiny and debate. Jubilees, with its detailed retelling of biblical history and its unique chronological framework, was included in the Ethiopian canon but was often viewed with skepticism by other traditions. The debates surrounding Jubilees centered on its historical authenticity, its theological implications, and its alignment with the canonical texts of other Christian traditions.

The Ethiopian Orthodox Church's canon also includes texts such as the "Shepherd of Hermas" and the "Epistle of Barnabas," which were excluded from the canonical lists of other Christian communities. The acceptance of these texts reflects the Ethiopian church's distinctive theological and ecclesiastical perspectives, as well as its historical commitment to preserving a broad and inclusive understanding of sacred scripture.

The process of canonization within the Ethiopian Orthodox Church was influenced by various factors, including ecclesiastical authority, theological considerations, and historical circumstances. The church's decisions regarding canonicity were not made in isolation but were part of a broader process of theological reflection and ecclesiastical deliberation that took place over centuries.

The disputes over canonicity were not limited to external influences but also involved internal theological debates within the Ethiopian Orthodox Church. Church scholars and leaders engaged in extensive discussions about the nature of scripture, the criteria for canonicity, and the theological significance of various texts. These debates were shaped by a deep commitment to preserving the integrity and purity of the Christian faith.

Throughout its history, the Ethiopian Orthodox Church has demonstrated a remarkable degree of continuity and resilience in its approach to canonization. Despite external pressures and theological disagreements, the church has maintained its commitment to its unique canon and has continued to venerate the additional texts that are integral to its tradition.

The historical debates over canonicity within the Ethiopian Orthodox Church highlight the complex and dynamic nature of scriptural interpretation and authority. These debates reflect a broader pattern of theological diversity and ecclesiastical discernment within

Christianity, underscoring the richness and complexity of the biblical tradition.

## Comparisons with Canonicity Disputes in Other Traditions

Comparing the Ethiopian Orthodox Church's disputes over canonicity with those in other Christian traditions reveals both similarities and differences in how various communities have approached the question of scriptural authority. The process of determining which texts should be included in the canon has been a central issue in Christian history, and the Ethiopian Orthodox experience offers valuable insights into these broader debates.

In the early church, debates over the canon were marked by significant diversity and contention. Different Christian communities had varying lists of accepted texts, reflecting a range of theological perspectives and historical influences. The Ethiopian Orthodox Church's canon, with its inclusion of additional texts, represents one of the more distinctive examples of early Christian diversity. This contrasts with the more streamlined canons that emerged in other traditions.

The Western Christian tradition, particularly within the Roman Catholic and Protestant churches, saw its own disputes over canonicity. The Protestant Reformation in the 16th century led to a reevaluation of the canon, resulting in the exclusion of several books from the Old Testament that were retained by the Roman Catholic Church. The Protestant canon, which excludes books such as Tobit, Judith, and Wisdom, contrasts sharply with the Ethiopian Orthodox canon, which includes many of these texts.

The Eastern Orthodox Church, while sharing some texts with the Ethiopian Orthodox tradition, also has its own unique canon. The Eastern Orthodox canon includes books such as 1 and 2 Maccabees and the Psalms of Solomon, which are not found in the Ethiopian canon. The debates within the Eastern Orthodox tradition, similar to those in Ethiopia, were shaped by theological, historical, and ecclesiastical considerations.

The debates over canonicity in the Ethiopian Orthodox Church also echo broader discussions in other early Christian communities. For example, the debates over the inclusion of the Apocryphal and Pseudepigraphal texts were not unique to Ethiopia but were also present in the early Christian discussions across the Mediterranean world. These debates often centered on issues of theological consistency, historical authenticity, and the authority of the texts.

In the Jewish tradition, the formation of the Hebrew Bible (Tanakh) involved its own complex process of determining which texts were considered authoritative. Similar to the Christian canon debates, Jewish discussions about scriptural authority involved theological, historical, and communal factors. The differences between the Jewish canon and Christian canons reflect divergent theological emphases and interpretive traditions.

The influence of historical and cultural contexts on canonicity debates is evident in both Ethiopian and other Christian traditions. The Ethiopian Orthodox Church's canon reflects its unique historical and cultural milieu, including its connections to ancient Jewish traditions and its own ecclesiastical history. Similarly, the canons of other Christian traditions were shaped by their specific historical and cultural contexts, influencing their approach to scriptural authority.

The process of canonization in the Ethiopian Orthodox Church, while distinct, shares common elements with other Christian traditions. Debates over canonicity often involve theological reflection, ecclesiastical authority, and historical research. These commonalities highlight the broader patterns of scriptural discernment that have characterized the history of Christianity.

The Ethiopian Orthodox Church's disputes over canonicity, when compared with those in other Christian traditions, offer valuable insights into the complex and diverse nature of biblical authority. The Ethiopian experience reflects both the unique aspects of its own tradition and the broader patterns of theological and historical debate that have shaped the development of the Christian canon.

# Chapter 14

# Modern Interpretive Debates

## Contemporary Theological and Scholarly Debates

The landscape of contemporary theological and scholarly debates is marked by a profound shift in how sacred texts and religious doctrines are understood. This shift is driven by various critical methodologies that have redefined the traditional interpretations of religious scriptures. One of the most significant developments in modern theology is the application of historical-critical methods to ancient texts. Scholars employing these methods analyze the socio-political, economic, and cultural contexts in which these texts were written. This approach seeks to uncover the original meanings and purposes of the scriptures, often leading to reinterpretations that diverge from long-standing traditional views.

Historical-critical scholarship challenges literal interpretations by considering how texts may have been edited or redacted over time. For instance, the Pentateuch, traditionally attributed to Moses, is now understood by many scholars to be a compilation of multiple sources written over centuries. This insight has led to debates about the historical accuracy of biblical accounts and the nature of divine inspiration. By examining textual variations and historical contexts, scholars provide a more nuanced understanding of the scriptures that can conflict with traditional beliefs.

Feminist theology has emerged as a transformative force in contemporary religious discourse. This perspective critiques traditional religious narratives for their androcentric biases, challenging patriarchal interpretations and seeking to highlight the roles and experiences of women in sacred texts. Feminist scholars argue that traditional readings often marginalize or distort the contributions of female figures in religious history. By reinterpreting these texts from a feminist perspective, they aim to promote gender equality and inclusivity within religious traditions.

Liberation theology represents another significant contemporary development, particularly in the context of social justice. Rooted in the struggles of marginalized and oppressed communities, liberation theology emphasizes the need for a theology that addresses systemic injustices and advocates for the poor and disenfranchised. This approach challenges traditional theological frameworks that may have been complicit in perpetuating social inequalities. Scholars within this tradition argue for a reinterpretation of scriptures that aligns with the principles of justice and human rights.

Interfaith dialogue has also become a crucial component of contemporary theological debates. In a globalized world, increased interaction between different religious traditions has highlighted both commonalities and differences. Interfaith discussions focus on fostering mutual understanding and respect, often leading to a reevaluation of exclusivist claims made by individual faith traditions. This dialogue encourages a more inclusive approach to religious practice and belief, emphasizing shared values and collaborative efforts toward common goals.

Postcolonial theology has emerged as a response to the legacy of colonialism and its impact on religious traditions. This perspective critiques the ways in which colonial powers have used religion as a tool of domination and seeks to reclaim indigenous and marginalized voices within theological discourse. Postcolonial scholars advocate for a more equitable and inclusive understanding of religious traditions that acknowledges the effects of colonialism and promotes decolonization.

The rise of digital technology and its impact on religious practice is another area of contemporary debate. The proliferation of online religious content and virtual communities has transformed how individuals engage with their faith. Scholars explore how digital platforms influence religious expression, community formation, and the dissemination of theological ideas. This raises questions about the authenticity and depth of online religious experiences compared to traditional forms of worship and community.

Queer theology is a relatively new field that challenges traditional understandings of sexuality and gender within religious contexts. This approach seeks to reexamine sacred texts and doctrines from a queer perspective, advocating for the inclusion and acceptance of LGBTQ+ individuals within religious communities. Queer theologians argue for a reinterpretation of texts that reflects a broader understanding of human diversity and rejects exclusionary practices.

Environmental theology addresses the growing concerns about ecological degradation and climate change. This perspective emphasizes the theological implications of humanity's relationship with the natural world and advocates for a stewardship ethic that prioritizes environmental sustainability. Scholars within this field argue for a reinterpretation of religious teachings to reflect the urgency of ecological issues and promote responsible environmental practices.

The impact of globalization on religious identity and practice is another critical area of contemporary debate. As cultures and religions intersect in increasingly complex ways, scholars examine how globalization affects religious beliefs and practices. This includes exploring the effects of cultural exchange, migration, and the spread of global religious movements. The resulting hybridization of religious practices raises questions about authenticity, tradition, and adaptation in a globalized world.

Secularization theory also plays a role in contemporary theological debates. This theory posits that modernity and rationalism lead to the decline of religious authority and practice. Scholars debate the implications of secularization for religious beliefs and institutions, considering whether secularization represents a decline in religiosity or a transformation of religious practice in the modern age. This debate influences how religious traditions adapt to contemporary challenges and changing societal values.

The relationship between science and religion continues to be a prominent topic in theological debates. As scientific knowledge advances, particularly in fields such as cosmology and evolutionary biology, questions arise about the compatibility of scientific explanations with religious beliefs. Scholars engage in discussions about whether science and religion can coexist harmoniously or if they represent fundamentally opposing worldviews. This dialogue impacts how religious traditions interpret scientific findings and integrate them into their understanding of the world.

## The Impact of Modern Scholarship on Traditional Beliefs

Modern scholarship has profoundly impacted traditional beliefs, often challenging long-held doctrines and practices. One of the most significant effects is the reexamination of sacred texts through historical-critical methods. Traditional literal interpretations are increasingly questioned as scholars apply rigorous analytical techniques to uncover the historical and cultural contexts of these texts. This has led to a more nuanced understanding of scriptures, prompting debates within religious communities about the validity of traditional interpretations.

The impact of feminist theology on traditional beliefs is particularly notable. By critiquing patriarchal interpretations and highlighting the roles of women in sacred texts, feminist scholars have prompted religious communities to reevaluate gender roles and practices. This has led to significant changes in many traditions, including the ordination of women and the reexamination of gendered language and teachings. Feminist theology challenges traditional beliefs by advocating for greater inclusivity and equality within religious practices.

Liberation theology has also reshaped traditional beliefs by emphasizing social justice and the plight of the marginalized. This perspective challenges traditional theological frameworks that may have supported or ignored systemic inequalities. The focus on addressing poverty, oppression, and injustice has led to a rethinking of religious doctrines and practices to align with principles of social equity and human rights.

Interfaith dialogue has impacted traditional beliefs by promoting a more inclusive and pluralistic approach to religion. As different faith traditions engage in dialogue, there is a growing emphasis on common values and mutual respect. This has led to a reevaluation of exclusivist claims and a greater openness to understanding and incorporating insights from other religious traditions. Interfaith dialogue challenges traditional beliefs by advocating for a more inclusive and cooperative approach to religious practice.

Postcolonial theology has influenced traditional beliefs by addressing the legacy of colonialism and its effects on religious traditions. This perspective critiques the ways in which colonial powers used religion as a tool of domination and seeks to reclaim marginalized voices within theological discourse. Postcolonial theology challenges traditional beliefs by promoting a more equitable and inclusive understanding of religion that acknowledges the impacts of colonialism.

Digital technology has transformed religious practice and belief in significant ways. The rise of online religious communities and virtual worship has changed how individuals engage with their faith. Scholars debate the impact of digital technology on religious authenticity and community, leading to a rethinking of traditional practices and the ways in which religious experiences are mediated through digital platforms. This shift challenges traditional beliefs about the nature and practice of religion in a digital age.

Queer theology has challenged traditional beliefs by reexamining sexuality and gender roles within religious contexts. By advocating for the inclusion of LGBTQ+ individuals and critiquing exclusionary practices, queer theology prompts religious communities to rethink traditional teachings and practices related to sexuality and gender. This has led to debates about the interpretation of sacred texts and the acceptance of diverse sexual and gender identities within religious traditions.

Environmental theology has influenced traditional beliefs by emphasizing the need for environmental stewardship and sustainability. This perspective challenges traditional beliefs about humanity's relationship with the natural world, advocating for a reinterpretation of religious teachings to address ecological concerns. The focus on environmental issues prompts religious communities to reconsider their practices and teachings in light of the urgency of climate change and environmental degradation.

Globalization has impacted traditional beliefs by introducing new cultural and religious influences. As global interactions increase, religious traditions encounter new ideas and practices that challenge traditional beliefs. The resulting hybridization of religious practices raises questions about authenticity and adaptation, leading to debates about how traditional beliefs can evolve in a globalized world while maintaining their core values.

Secularization theory has influenced traditional beliefs by suggesting that modernity and rationalism lead to a decline in religious authority. Scholars debate whether secularization represents a decline in religiosity or a transformation of religious practice. This discussion affects how traditional beliefs are understood and practiced in a secularized world, prompting religious communities to adapt their teachings and practices to contemporary societal values.

The relationship between science and religion continues to be a critical area of impact on traditional beliefs. As scientific knowledge advances, questions arise about how scientific explanations align with or challenge religious doctrines. The dialogue between science and religion influences how traditional beliefs are interpreted in light of scientific discoveries, leading to ongoing debates about the compatibility of faith and reason.

# Chapter 15

# Efforts to Digitize and Increase Accessibility

## Projects and Initiatives to Preserve and Digitize Manuscripts

The preservation and digitization of manuscripts is a crucial undertaking for safeguarding historical and cultural heritage. In recent years, numerous projects and initiatives have emerged globally to address the challenge of preserving fragile manuscripts and making them accessible through digital means. These efforts are driven by the recognition that many manuscripts are at risk of deterioration due to age, environmental conditions, and physical handling.

One prominent example is the Digitizing Manuscripts Project undertaken by major libraries and archives worldwide. Institutions such as the British Library and the Library of Congress have launched initiatives to digitize their extensive collections of manuscripts. These projects often involve high-resolution scanning and the use of advanced imaging technologies to capture the intricate details of each manuscript. The digital images are then stored in online databases, providing researchers and the public with access to previously inaccessible materials.

In addition to large institutional projects, there are numerous smaller-scale initiatives focused on specific types of manuscripts or regional collections. For instance, the Medieval Manuscripts Project at the University of Oxford aims to digitize and preserve medieval manuscripts housed in the Bodleian Library. This project not only involves digitization but also the development of detailed cataloging and metadata systems to enhance searchability and scholarly research.

Another significant effort is the Endangered Archives Programme, funded by the British Library. This initiative supports projects around the world that focus on preserving and digitizing endangered archival materials.

The program provides grants to institutions and individuals working on preserving manuscripts that are at risk of being lost due to neglect, conflict, or natural disasters. Projects funded by this program include digitizing ancient manuscripts from the Middle East, Africa, and Asia.

The digitization of manuscripts also includes efforts to make texts available in multiple languages and formats. The Rosetta Project, for example, aims to digitize and archive languages and texts that are endangered or have limited digital representation. By creating digital archives that include translations and linguistic analyses, this initiative helps preserve the linguistic diversity of manuscript collections.

Crowdsourcing is another innovative approach to manuscript preservation and digitization. Platforms like the Transcribe Bentham Project invite volunteers to transcribe and encode historical manuscripts. This collaborative effort not only accelerates the digitization process but also engages the public in preserving historical documents. The transcriptions are then incorporated into digital archives, enhancing accessibility and scholarly research.

Digital preservation also involves the use of advanced technologies to ensure the long-term viability of digital records. The National Digital Preservation Program, for example, focuses on developing strategies and tools for preserving digital content over time. This includes addressing issues related to data storage, migration, and format obsolescence to ensure that digitized manuscripts remain accessible for future generations.

Collaborative international initiatives further amplify the impact of digitization projects. The World Digital Library, for instance, is a joint effort by UNESCO and various national libraries to provide access to significant cultural documents from around the world. By digitizing and making available manuscripts, maps, and other historical documents, the World Digital Library aims to promote global cultural understanding and research.

In addition to these initiatives, there are specialized projects focused on specific manuscript collections. For example, the Dead Sea Scrolls Digital Library, managed by the Israel Antiquities Authority, has digitized and made accessible the ancient manuscripts discovered in the Qumran Caves. This project provides high-resolution images and detailed scholarly analyses of the scrolls, facilitating research and study.

The preservation of manuscripts also involves addressing the challenges of physical deterioration. Projects often include conservation efforts such as restoring damaged manuscripts, improving storage conditions, and developing protective enclosures. These measures ensure that manuscripts are not only digitized but also preserved in their physical form for future study.

Educational outreach and training are integral components of manuscript digitization projects. Many initiatives include programs to train librarians, archivists, and researchers in best practices for digitization and preservation. By sharing knowledge and expertise, these programs help build capacity within institutions and communities involved in manuscript preservation.

## Efforts to Make the Ethiopian Orthodox Bible Accessible to a Global Audience

The Ethiopian Orthodox Bible is a crucial component of the Ethiopian Orthodox Church's heritage, encompassing a unique canon that includes texts not found in other Christian traditions. Efforts to make this important religious text accessible to a global audience involve a combination of digitization, translation, and educational initiatives.

One of the primary efforts to increase global accessibility is the digitization of Ethiopian Orthodox manuscripts. Projects such as the Ethiopian Manuscript Imaging Project aim to preserve and digitize the ancient manuscripts of the Ethiopian Orthodox Bible. By using high-resolution imaging techniques, these projects capture detailed images of the manuscripts, which are then made available through online platforms. This digitization process ensures that the texts are preserved for future generations and accessible to scholars and the public worldwide.

In addition to digitization, translation efforts play a crucial role in making the Ethiopian Orthodox Bible accessible. Many of the texts are written in Ge'ez, an ancient liturgical language of Ethiopia, which is not widely understood outside of the Ethiopian Orthodox community. Translation projects work to provide translations of these texts into major world languages, such as English, French, and Spanish. These translations are essential for scholars, theologians, and general readers who wish to study and understand the unique aspects of the Ethiopian Orthodox canon.

The Ethiopian Orthodox Church has also engaged in outreach efforts to share its religious heritage with a broader audience. This includes creating educational resources and providing information about the Ethiopian Orthodox Bible's significance and history. By producing books, articles, and multimedia content, the Church aims to raise awareness about the richness of its tradition and encourage greater interest and understanding among global audiences.

Collaborations between Ethiopian scholars and international researchers have further advanced efforts to make the Ethiopian Orthodox Bible accessible. Joint research projects and academic conferences provide opportunities for scholars from different backgrounds to discuss and disseminate findings related to the Ethiopian Orthodox canon. These collaborations help bridge the gap between Ethiopian and global scholarship, fostering greater appreciation and understanding of the texts.

Institutions such as the Ethiopian Orthodox Tewahedo Church's Central Synod have played a key role in facilitating the global dissemination of the Bible. By supporting digitization and translation initiatives, these institutions ensure that the Ethiopian Orthodox Bible is represented accurately and comprehensively in international academic and religious discussions.

Museums and cultural organizations also contribute to the global accessibility of the Ethiopian Orthodox Bible through exhibitions and educational programs. These institutions often showcase manuscripts, artifacts, and historical materials related to the Ethiopian Orthodox tradition, providing context and fostering greater appreciation of the Bible's significance.

Online platforms and digital libraries have become vital tools for increasing access to the Ethiopian Orthodox Bible. Websites dedicated to religious texts and historical documents often include sections on Ethiopian Orthodox manuscripts, offering digital versions and scholarly resources. These platforms provide a convenient and accessible means for researchers and enthusiasts to explore the Bible's contents.

Efforts to preserve and promote the Ethiopian Orthodox Bible also involve addressing the challenges of maintaining and restoring physical manuscripts. Conservation projects focus on repairing and preserving damaged manuscripts, ensuring that they remain available for future digitization and study. This work is essential for protecting the integrity of the texts and supporting ongoing research.

Educational institutions and religious organizations are increasingly incorporating the Ethiopian Orthodox Bible into their curricula and programs. By offering courses, seminars, and workshops on Ethiopian Orthodox theology and scripture, these institutions help foster a deeper understanding of the Bible's significance and its place within the broader Christian tradition.

Publications and academic journals dedicated to religious studies often include research on the Ethiopian Orthodox Bible, furthering its global visibility. Articles, books, and essays contribute to the academic discourse surrounding the text, exploring its historical, theological, and cultural dimensions.

Efforts to digitize and increase the accessibility of manuscripts, including the Ethiopian Orthodox Bible, represent a significant commitment to preserving and sharing cultural and religious heritage. Through digitization, translation, collaboration, and education, these initiatives ensure that important texts are available to a global audience, fostering greater understanding and appreciation of diverse religious traditions.

# Chapter 16

# Spiritual Wisdom and Insights

## Key Spiritual Teachings and Insights from the Ethiopian Orthodox Bible

The Ethiopian Orthodox Bible, a cornerstone of the Ethiopian Orthodox Tewahedo Church, is rich with spiritual teachings and insights that have shaped the faith and practice of its adherents for centuries. This biblical canon includes texts both familiar and unique to the Ethiopian Orthodox tradition, offering a wealth of spiritual wisdom and guidance.

One of the key spiritual teachings found in the Ethiopian Orthodox Bible is the concept of divine providence and the sovereignty of God. This theme is prevalent throughout the texts, underscoring the belief that God is the ultimate ruler and sustainer of the universe. The teachings emphasize that God's providence governs all aspects of creation and human life, reassuring believers that they are under the care of a benevolent and omnipotent deity. This perspective encourages trust and faith in God's plans, even in times of adversity.

Another significant teaching is the emphasis on the transformative power of repentance and forgiveness. The Ethiopian Orthodox Bible highlights the importance of repentance as a means of reconciliation with God. Stories such as those of King David and the Prophet Jonah illustrate the process of seeking forgiveness and the profound change that occurs when one genuinely repents. This teaching encourages believers to pursue repentance sincerely and to offer forgiveness to others, reflecting the mercy and compassion of God.

The Ethiopian Orthodox Bible also emphasizes the importance of love and compassion in the life of a believer. The teachings frequently highlight the commandment to love one's neighbor, reflecting the belief that love is central to the practice of faith. The Epistle of James, included in the Ethiopian canon, underscores the importance of acting on one's faith through deeds of love and kindness. This teaching serves as a guiding principle for ethical behavior and interpersonal relationships.

The theme of spiritual warfare is another prominent teaching within the Ethiopian Orthodox Bible. This concept refers to the ongoing struggle between good and evil forces, both external and internal. The teachings often depict the Christian life as a battle against sin and temptation, encouraging believers to rely on prayer, faith, and the power of God to overcome spiritual challenges. The imagery of spiritual warfare serves as a reminder of the need for vigilance and spiritual strength.

Wisdom literature, such as the Book of Proverbs and the Book of Wisdom, offers profound insights into the nature of wisdom and its role in guiding human conduct. These texts emphasize that true wisdom comes from God and is essential for living a righteous and fulfilling life. The teachings encourage believers to seek wisdom through prayer, study, and reflection, recognizing that divine wisdom provides direction and understanding in all aspects of life.

The Ethiopian Orthodox Bible also places a strong emphasis on the importance of community and communal worship. The teachings highlight the significance of gathering for worship, participating in the sacraments, and supporting one another in the faith. The communal aspect of worship and fellowship is seen as essential for spiritual growth and the nurturing of a vibrant Christian community.

The concept of theosis, or deification, is a distinctive teaching within the Ethiopian Orthodox tradition. The Ethiopian Orthodox Bible reflects the belief that believers are called to become partakers of the divine nature through their union with Christ. This teaching emphasizes the transformative power of divine grace and the ultimate goal of becoming one with God. Theosis is seen as the culmination of the Christian journey and the fulfillment of God's purpose for humanity.

The Ethiopian Orthodox Bible also addresses the importance of humility and meekness as fundamental virtues. Teachings on humility highlight the need to recognize one's limitations and to approach others with a spirit of service and gentleness. The example of Christ's humility and the teachings of the Sermon on the Mount reinforce the value of humility as a path to spiritual growth and interpersonal harmony.

The notion of stewardship and responsible care for creation is another significant teaching. The Ethiopian Orthodox Bible underscores the responsibility of humanity to care for the earth and its resources as a reflection of God's creation. This teaching encourages believers to practice environmental stewardship and to use their resources wisely and ethically.

The Ethiopian Orthodox Bible also includes teachings on the nature of prayer and its role in the life of a believer. The texts emphasize the importance of persistent and heartfelt prayer as a means of communicating with God, seeking guidance, and expressing gratitude. The practice of prayer is seen as central to spiritual life and growth, fostering a deeper relationship with God.

The teachings on the afterlife and eternal life are integral to the Ethiopian Orthodox Bible. These teachings provide insights into the nature of life after death, emphasizing the hope of resurrection and eternal communion with God. The texts offer comfort and assurance to believers, reinforcing the promise of everlasting life and the ultimate fulfillment of God's plan for creation.

The Ethiopian Orthodox Bible also highlights the role of asceticism and spiritual discipline in the Christian life. Teachings on ascetic practices, such as fasting and self-denial, are seen as means of spiritual purification and growth. These practices are intended to help believers overcome worldly distractions and focus on their spiritual journey.

Finally, the Ethiopian Orthodox Bible emphasizes the significance of the sacraments and their role in the life of the Church. The sacraments, including baptism, Eucharist, and confession, are seen as essential means of receiving divine grace and participating in the life of Christ. The teachings underscore the importance of the sacraments in nurturing spiritual growth and maintaining a connection with the divine.

## The Relevance of These Teachings in Contemporary Life

The teachings and insights from the Ethiopian Orthodox Bible continue to hold significant relevance in contemporary life, offering guidance and wisdom for navigating the complexities of modern existence. As individuals and communities face various challenges, these ancient teachings provide a framework for addressing contemporary issues with spiritual depth and insight.

The concept of divine providence remains profoundly relevant in today's world, where uncertainty and instability are prevalent. In times of personal and societal challenges, the assurance of God's sovereignty and care can offer comfort and hope. Believers can draw strength from the teaching that God governs all aspects of life and trust in divine plans, even when faced with difficulties.

The emphasis on repentance and forgiveness speaks directly to the contemporary need for reconciliation and healing. In a world marked by conflict and division, the call to seek forgiveness and extend it to others is a powerful reminder of the importance of repairing relationships and fostering understanding. This teaching encourages individuals to address grievances and pursue peace, reflecting the transformative power of reconciliation.

The call to love and compassion is increasingly pertinent in a globalized world where interpersonal connections and social responsibility are vital. The teachings on love challenge individuals to practice empathy, kindness, and support in their interactions with others. This relevance is evident in efforts to address social injustices, promote inclusivity, and build compassionate communities.

The concept of spiritual warfare offers valuable insights for confronting the challenges of modern life. The struggle against sin and temptation is a universal experience, and the teachings on spiritual warfare provide strategies for overcoming personal and ethical struggles. This perspective encourages believers to remain vigilant and resilient in their spiritual journey, drawing strength from faith and prayer.

Wisdom literature from the Ethiopian Orthodox Bible provides timeless guidance for making sound decisions and living with integrity. In an age characterized by rapid change and complex choices, the emphasis on seeking divine wisdom remains crucial. The teachings encourage individuals to seek understanding through reflection, prayer, and study, applying divine wisdom to contemporary situations.

The importance of community and communal worship is particularly relevant in a world where social isolation and fragmentation are common. The teachings on communal worship highlight the value of connection, support, and shared faith. Engaging in communal activities and fostering relationships within a faith community contribute to spiritual well-being and a sense of belonging.

The doctrine of theosis, or deification, offers a transformative vision for personal growth and fulfillment. The aspiration to become one with God provides a framework for understanding the ultimate purpose of human life. In contemporary contexts, this teaching encourages individuals to pursue spiritual growth and strive for a deeper relationship with the divine.

Humility and meekness, as emphasized in the Ethiopian Orthodox Bible, are essential virtues for navigating contemporary social dynamics. In a culture often characterized by competition and self-promotion, the teachings on humility offer a countercultural perspective. Practicing humility fosters respectful interactions and promotes a spirit of service and cooperation.

Stewardship and responsible care for creation are increasingly urgent in the face of environmental challenges. The teachings on stewardship encourage individuals to take an active role in protecting and preserving the natural world. This perspective aligns with contemporary efforts to address environmental issues and promote sustainable practices.

The significance of prayer in contemporary life is evident as individuals seek spiritual connection and guidance amidst a busy and often stressful world. The teachings on prayer highlight its role in fostering a relationship with God and finding solace in times of need. Embracing a consistent practice of prayer can provide comfort and clarity in navigating life's challenges.

The teachings on the afterlife offer hope and reassurance in the face of existential questions and concerns about mortality. The promise of eternal life and resurrection provides a perspective that transcends the temporal nature of earthly existence. This hope can inspire individuals to live with a sense of purpose and to focus on spiritual goals.

Asceticism and spiritual discipline remain relevant as practices for cultivating inner growth and resilience. In a society that often emphasizes materialism and instant gratification, the teachings on ascetic practices offer an alternative approach. Engaging in spiritual disciplines such as fasting and reflection can help individuals develop self-control and focus on their spiritual journey.

The importance of the sacraments in contemporary life underscores their role in sustaining spiritual vitality and connection with the divine. The ongoing practice of sacraments such as baptism and Eucharist continues to be central to religious life, providing a means of receiving divine grace and participating in the communal life of the Church.

The teachings and insights from the Ethiopian Orthodox Bible offer profound relevance to contemporary life. By addressing personal, social, and spiritual challenges, these ancient teachings provide a framework for living with faith, compassion, and wisdom in the modern world.

# Chapter 17

# Historical Significance and Scholarly Importance

## The Bible's Status as the Oldest Surviving Bible

The Ethiopian Orthodox Bible, particularly the Garima Gospels, holds the distinction of being one of the oldest surviving illustrated Christian Bibles. Its historical significance is unparalleled, reflecting the rich religious and cultural heritage of Ethiopia. The Garima Gospels, believed to have been created around the 5th or 6th century, are among the earliest complete illuminated Christian manuscripts, predating other known gospel books such as the Lindisfarne Gospels and the Book of Kells.

The Garima Gospels are named after Abba Garima, a 6th-century monk who is said to have arrived in Ethiopia from Constantinople. According to legend, Abba Garima completed the entire manuscript in a single day with divine assistance. While this legend adds a mystical dimension to the manuscripts, their historical and artistic value is beyond dispute. The Garima Gospels are preserved in the Abba Garima Monastery in northern Ethiopia, providing a tangible link to the early Christian period in Africa.

The Ethiopian Orthodox Bible's status as the oldest surviving Bible is not limited to the Garima Gospels. The broader Ethiopian biblical canon, including the Orit (Old Testament) and the New Testament, comprises texts that have been meticulously preserved and transmitted through centuries. This canon includes books not found in other Christian Bibles, such as the Book of Enoch and the Book of Jubilees, reflecting the unique theological and historical development of Ethiopian Christianity.

The preservation of these texts in Ge'ez, the ancient liturgical language of Ethiopia, further underscores their historical significance. Ge'ez, no longer spoken as a vernacular language, remains the liturgical language of the Ethiopian Orthodox Tewahedo Church. The use of Ge'ez in the manuscripts connects contemporary Ethiopian worship with its ancient roots, maintaining a continuous link to the early Christian tradition.

The physical condition of these ancient manuscripts, some of which have survived in remarkable condition despite their age, provides invaluable insights into the materials and techniques used by early scribes and artists. The manuscripts are made of parchment, a durable material made from animal skin, and are often richly decorated with intricate illuminations and vibrant colors. The preservation of these manuscripts offers a glimpse into the artistic and cultural practices of the time.

The Ethiopian Orthodox Bible's ancient manuscripts also reflect the cross-cultural interactions that have shaped Ethiopian Christianity. Influences from Byzantine, Coptic, and Syrian Christian traditions are evident in the artistic styles and textual traditions of the manuscripts. These cross-cultural exchanges highlight Ethiopia's historical role as a hub of Christian scholarship and art, bridging different Christian traditions.

The discovery and study of the Garima Gospels and other ancient Ethiopian manuscripts have significantly contributed to the understanding of early Christian art and iconography. The illuminations in these manuscripts provide some of the earliest examples of Christian art, depicting biblical scenes and figures with a distinct Ethiopian style. These artworks offer a unique perspective on the development of Christian iconography and its adaptation to different cultural contexts.

The Ethiopian Orthodox Bible's historical significance extends beyond its artistic and textual value. It also plays a crucial role in understanding the development of Christian doctrine and liturgy. The inclusion of unique texts and the specific ordering of the canon reflect the theological priorities and liturgical practices of the Ethiopian Orthodox Church. Studying these aspects provides insights into the diversity of early Christian thought and practice.

The Ethiopian Orthodox Bible's status as one of the oldest surviving Bibles has attracted considerable scholarly attention. Researchers from various fields, including theology, history, art history, and linguistics, have studied these manuscripts to gain a deeper understanding of early Christian history and the development of biblical texts. The manuscripts serve as primary sources for scholars seeking to reconstruct the early history of the Bible and its transmission.

The preservation of the Ethiopian Orthodox Bible and its manuscripts is a testament to the dedication and reverence of the Ethiopian Orthodox Tewahedo Church and its faithful. The efforts to protect and maintain these ancient texts through centuries of political and social changes highlight the central role of the Bible in Ethiopian religious and cultural identity. This enduring commitment ensures that the spiritual and historical heritage contained within these manuscripts continues to be accessible to future generations.

The Ethiopian Orthodox Bible's ancient manuscripts are not only valuable for their content but also for the context they provide about the communities that produced and preserved them. The study of these manuscripts sheds light on the monastic communities, scribes, and artists who contributed to their creation. Understanding the social and religious contexts of these communities enhances the appreciation of the manuscripts as living documents that reflect the faith and devotion of generations.

The Ethiopian Orthodox Bible's historical significance is also evident in its influence on Ethiopian literature and culture. The Bible has inspired a rich tradition of religious poetry, hymns, and theological writings in Ge'ez and later in Amharic, the modern liturgical language. This literary heritage continues to be a source of spiritual inspiration and cultural pride for Ethiopians, illustrating the profound impact of the Bible on the nation's identity.

The Ethiopian Orthodox Bible's status as one of the oldest surviving Bibles is a testament to its historical and cultural significance. Its ancient manuscripts, including the Garima Gospels, provide invaluable insights into early Christian art, theology, and liturgy. The preservation and study of these texts offer a unique window into the rich religious heritage of Ethiopia and its enduring influence on Christian scholarship and culture.

## Its Importance for Scholars of Religion, History, and Culture

The Ethiopian Orthodox Bible holds immense importance for scholars across various disciplines, including religion, history, and culture. Its unique textual tradition and ancient manuscripts provide a wealth of information that contributes to a deeper understanding of early Christianity, the development of biblical texts, and the cultural exchanges that have shaped religious traditions.

For scholars of religion, the Ethiopian Orthodox Bible offers a distinctive perspective on Christian theology and practice. The inclusion of texts not found in other Christian canons, such as the Book of Enoch and the Book of Jubilees, provides valuable insights into the diversity of early Christian thought. These texts, often categorized as part of the "Old Testament Pseudepigrapha," shed light on theological themes, eschatological beliefs, and ethical teachings that were influential in the early Christian world.

The Ethiopian Orthodox Bible's unique canon also includes additional books in the Old Testament, such as 1 Esdras, 2 Esdras, and the Prayer of Manasseh. These texts offer scholars an expanded view of the scriptural landscape of early Christianity, revealing how different communities valued and interpreted various writings. Studying these texts helps scholars understand the processes of canon formation and the criteria used by different Christian traditions to determine their authoritative scriptures.

The preservation of the Ethiopian Orthodox Bible in Ge'ez, an ancient Semitic language, provides linguistic scholars with a valuable resource for studying the development of this language and its role in the religious and cultural life of Ethiopia. Ge'ez is no longer spoken as a vernacular language, but it remains the liturgical language of the Ethiopian Orthodox Church. The study of Ge'ez manuscripts contributes to the understanding of the linguistic and literary history of Ethiopia and the broader Semitic language family.

The Ethiopian Orthodox Bible's manuscripts are also of great interest to historians studying the history of Christianity in Africa. Ethiopia's adoption of Christianity in the 4th century makes it one of the oldest Christian nations in the world. The Bible's manuscripts provide direct evidence of the early spread and establishment of Christianity in Ethiopia, offering insights into the region's religious, cultural, and political history. These texts help historians reconstruct the interactions between Ethiopia and other early Christian communities, including those in the Mediterranean and Near East.

For art historians, the Ethiopian Orthodox Bible's illuminated manuscripts are a treasure trove of information about early Christian art and iconography. The vibrant and intricate illuminations in the Garima Gospels and other manuscripts showcase the artistic traditions of Ethiopian Christianity. These artworks provide examples of how biblical themes and figures were depicted in different cultural contexts, contributing to the broader understanding of the development of Christian art.

The study of the Ethiopian Orthodox Bible also enhances the understanding of monasticism and its role in preserving and transmitting religious texts. Ethiopian monasteries have been centers of religious scholarship and manuscript production for centuries. The manuscripts reflect the devotional practices, theological debates, and intellectual endeavors of monastic communities. Scholars studying these aspects gain insights into the daily life and spiritual pursuits of

Ethiopian monks and their contributions to Christian literature.

Cultural anthropologists and ethnographers find the Ethiopian Orthodox Bible's manuscripts valuable for understanding the cultural and religious identity of Ethiopian communities. The Bible has played a central role in shaping the beliefs, rituals, and social structures of Ethiopian society. The study of these manuscripts reveals how religious texts influence cultural practices, social norms, and communal identities. This interdisciplinary approach provides a holistic view of the interplay between religion and culture.

The Ethiopian Orthodox Bible's ancient manuscripts also contribute to the study of textual transmission and manuscript preservation. The physical condition of the manuscripts, the materials used, and the techniques of production provide important information about the historical context of their creation. Scholars studying these aspects gain insights into the methods of manuscript production, the challenges of preservation, and the historical circumstances that influenced the survival of these texts.

The Ethiopian Orthodox Bible's significance extends to the field of comparative religion. The unique texts and theological perspectives found in the Ethiopian canon provide a valuable point of comparison with other Christian and religious traditions. Comparative studies reveal the diversity of religious thought and practice in the early Christian world and highlight the contributions of Ethiopian Christianity to the broader religious landscape.

The interdisciplinary study of the Ethiopian Orthodox Bible also fosters international scholarly collaboration. Researchers from different fields and backgrounds come together to study these manuscripts, sharing expertise and insights. This collaborative approach enriches the understanding of the Ethiopian Orthodox Bible and its broader historical and cultural context, promoting cross-cultural and interfaith dialogue.

The Ethiopian Orthodox Bible's manuscripts are also significant for their impact on modern religious practices and beliefs. The continued use of these texts in Ethiopian Orthodox worship and their influence on contemporary theological discussions demonstrate the enduring relevance of this ancient biblical tradition. Scholars studying these aspects gain insights into how historical texts shape and inform modern religious experiences.

The Ethiopian Orthodox Bible holds immense importance for scholars of religion, history, and culture. Its unique textual tradition and ancient manuscripts provide valuable insights into early Christian theology, the development of biblical texts, linguistic history, and the cultural exchanges that have shaped religious traditions. The interdisciplinary study of these manuscripts enhances the understanding of the rich religious heritage of Ethiopia and its contributions to the broader Christian and scholarly communities.

# Chapter 18

# Liturgical Celebrations and Manuscript Illumination

## The Role of the Bible in Ethiopian Liturgical Practices

The Ethiopian Orthodox Bible plays a central and vital role in the liturgical practices of the Ethiopian Orthodox Tewahedo Church. The Bible is not merely a text to be read but a living document that informs and shapes the worship, rituals, and daily practices of the faithful. The liturgy of the Ethiopian Orthodox Church is deeply rooted in biblical texts, and every aspect of the church's worship is imbued with scripture.

At the heart of Ethiopian liturgical practice is the Divine Liturgy, or Qidase, which is the Eucharistic celebration. The Qidase is a profound and elaborate service that incorporates numerous readings from both the Old and New Testaments. These readings are carefully selected to correspond with the liturgical calendar and the specific feast being celebrated. The scripture readings form the backbone of the service, guiding the prayers, hymns, and rituals that unfold during the liturgy.

The Ethiopian Orthodox Bible is also integral to the celebration of the various sacraments, or Mysteries, of the Church. Baptism, Chrismation, Confession, Holy Orders, Matrimony, and Anointing of the Sick all involve the use of scripture. For example, during the sacrament of Baptism, passages from the Gospels and the Epistles are read to underscore the spiritual rebirth and the new life in Christ that the sacrament signifies. Similarly, during Matrimony, readings from the Epistles and the Gospels highlight the sanctity and divine purpose of marriage.

One of the most distinctive aspects of Ethiopian liturgical practice is the extensive use of the Psalms. The Book of Psalms, known as the Zämäre Däwit, is a fundamental component of daily worship and personal devotion. The Psalms are recited and chanted at various times throughout the day, particularly during the canonical hours, which include services like Matins (Morning Prayer), Vespers (Evening Prayer), and Compline (Night Prayer). The rhythmic and melodic chanting of the Psalms creates a spiritual atmosphere that elevates the worship experience.

The Ethiopian Orthodox liturgical calendar is rich with feasts and fasts, many of which are rooted in biblical events and figures. Major feasts such as Timkat (Epiphany), Fasika (Easter), and Meskel (Finding of the True Cross) are celebrated with grand liturgical ceremonies that prominently feature scripture readings and hymns inspired by biblical texts. These celebrations not only commemorate historical events but also serve as a means of re-living and participating in the sacred history recounted in the Bible.

The Bible also plays a significant role in the homiletic tradition of the Ethiopian Orthodox Church. Sermons delivered by clergy during liturgical services are deeply rooted in biblical exegesis. These sermons aim to elucidate the meaning of the scripture readings, offering moral and spiritual guidance to the congregation. The homilies help bridge the gap between the ancient biblical texts and the contemporary lives of the faithful, making the teachings of the Bible relevant to their daily experiences.

The use of the Bible in Ethiopian liturgical practices is not limited to public worship but extends to personal and family devotions. Many Ethiopian Orthodox Christians maintain a daily practice of reading and reflecting on scripture. Family prayers and rituals often involve reading passages from the Bible, particularly the Gospels and the Psalms. This practice fosters a deep and personal connection with the sacred texts, reinforcing their central role in the spiritual lives of the faithful.

The Ethiopian Orthodox Bible is also central to the monastic tradition. Monasteries, which have been centers of religious life and scholarship for centuries, place a strong emphasis on the study and recitation of scripture. Monks and nuns dedicate significant portions of their day to reading, chanting, and meditating on the Bible. The rigorous and disciplined engagement with scripture is seen as a means of spiritual purification and enlightenment.

In addition to its liturgical and devotional uses, the Bible is also a source of inspiration for the rich hymnographic tradition of the Ethiopian Orthodox Church. The Church has a vast repertoire of hymns, known as Zema, which are sung during liturgical services and feasts. Many of these hymns draw directly from biblical texts or are inspired by biblical themes. The hymns serve to reinforce the teachings of the Bible and to create an immersive worship experience that engages both the mind and the heart.

The role of the Bible in Ethiopian liturgical practices is further highlighted by the practice of processions. During major feasts and celebrations, the clergy and the faithful participate in processions where the Gospel book, often richly decorated, is carried and venerated. These processions symbolize the presence of the Word of God in the midst of the community and serve as a public witness to the centrality of the Bible in the life of the Church.

The Ethiopian Orthodox Church also places great importance on the memorization of scripture. From a young age, children are encouraged to memorize passages from the Bible, particularly the Psalms and key verses from the Gospels. This practice not only aids in the internalization of the scriptures but also ensures that the sacred texts are readily available to the faithful in their daily lives, even in contexts where printed Bibles may not be accessible.

The Bible's role in Ethiopian liturgical practices is deeply intertwined with the Church's theological framework. The Ethiopian Orthodox Tewahedo Church holds to a Christocentric interpretation of scripture, viewing the entire Bible as a unified narrative that culminates in the incarnation, life, death, and resurrection of Jesus Christ. This theological perspective shapes the way scripture is read and understood in the liturgy, emphasizing the continuity between the Old and New Testaments and the fulfillment of God's promises in Christ.

The Ethiopian Orthodox Bible is central to the liturgical practices of the Ethiopian Orthodox Tewahedo Church. Its use in public worship, sacraments, personal devotions, monastic life, hymnography, processions, and theological interpretation underscores its profound significance. The Bible is not merely a text to be read but a living document that shapes and defines the spiritual life of the Ethiopian Orthodox community.

## The Art and Significance of Illuminated Manuscripts

The illuminated manuscripts of the Ethiopian Orthodox Bible are among the most treasured artifacts of Ethiopian Christian culture. These manuscripts are renowned for their intricate artistry, vibrant colors, and detailed illuminations, which serve not only as decorations but as visual interpretations of the sacred texts. The art of manuscript illumination in Ethiopia reflects a rich tradition that combines religious devotion, artistic skill, and cultural heritage.

Illuminated manuscripts in the Ethiopian Orthodox tradition often include elaborate frontispieces, decorated initials, and miniature paintings that illustrate scenes from the Bible. These artistic elements are not merely ornamental; they play a crucial role in conveying the spiritual and theological messages of the texts. The illuminations serve as visual aids that enhance the reader's understanding and meditation on the scripture, making the sacred narratives more accessible and engaging.

The process of creating illuminated manuscripts in Ethiopia is a meticulous and devotional practice. Scribes and artists, often monks, dedicate years to the production of a single manuscript. The materials used, including parchment made from animal skins, natural pigments for the inks and paints, and gold leaf for gilding, reflect the high value placed on these sacred texts. The painstaking effort invested in these manuscripts underscores their importance as objects of reverence and veneration.

One of the most striking features of Ethiopian illuminated manuscripts is their use of color. The vibrant reds, blues, greens, and golds create a sense of awe and wonder, drawing the viewer into the sacred world of the scriptures. The colors are not chosen randomly; they often carry symbolic meanings that enhance the spiritual message of the illuminations. For example, gold is frequently used to symbolize divine light and glory, while red may represent the blood of Christ and the martyrs.

The iconography in Ethiopian illuminated manuscripts is rich with symbolic imagery that reflects the theological and cultural context of Ethiopian Christianity. Common themes include depictions of Christ, the Virgin Mary, angels, and saints, as well as scenes from the Old and New Testaments. The artistic style is characterized by a distinctive Ethiopian aesthetic, with elongated figures, expressive faces, and intricate patterns. This unique style distinguishes Ethiopian manuscripts from those of other Christian traditions.

The significance of illuminated manuscripts extends beyond their aesthetic beauty. They are also invaluable historical documents that provide insights into the religious, cultural, and social life of Ethiopia throughout the centuries. The manuscripts often include colophons, or inscriptions by the scribes, which record the date of completion, the names of the patrons, and other historical details. These colophons offer valuable information about the context in which the manuscripts were produced and used.

Illuminated manuscripts also play a crucial role in the transmission and preservation of the Ethiopian Orthodox Bible. The process of copying and illuminating manuscripts ensured the continuity and accuracy of the biblical texts over generations. The manuscripts were often housed in monasteries and churches, where they were carefully preserved and protected. This tradition of manuscript production and preservation has helped to maintain the integrity of the Ethiopian biblical canon and its unique textual variants.

The illuminated manuscripts of the Ethiopian Orthodox Bible are not only important for their religious and historical value but also for their contribution to the field of art history. The study of these manuscripts provides insights into the development of Christian art in Ethiopia and its interactions with other artistic traditions. The manuscripts reveal the influences of Byzantine, Coptic, and Islamic art, reflecting Ethiopia's position as a crossroads of cultural exchange.

In contemporary times, the illuminated manuscripts of the Ethiopian Orthodox Bible continue to inspire artists and scholars alike. Exhibitions of these manuscripts in museums and galleries around the world have brought greater awareness of Ethiopia's rich artistic heritage. The intricate beauty and spiritual depth of the illuminations captivate viewers, fostering a deeper appreciation for the religious and cultural significance of these works of art.

The significance of illuminated manuscripts in Ethiopian Christianity is also reflected in their role in liturgical celebrations. During major feasts and processions, illuminated gospel books are carried and venerated as symbols of the presence of the Word of God. The visual splendor of the manuscripts enhances the solemnity and joy of these celebrations, creating a tangible connection between the sacred text and the worshiping community.

In addition to their liturgical use, illuminated manuscripts are also studied and revered in theological education. Seminaries and religious schools in Ethiopia use these manuscripts as teaching tools, allowing students to engage with the scripture in both its textual and visual dimensions. The study of illuminated manuscripts fosters a holistic understanding of the Bible, integrating theological, historical, and artistic perspectives.

The preservation of illuminated manuscripts remains a priority for the Ethiopian Orthodox Church and cultural heritage organizations. Efforts to conserve and digitize these manuscripts are crucial for ensuring their accessibility to future generations. Digitalization projects not only preserve the physical integrity of the manuscripts but also make them available to a global audience, promoting wider recognition and appreciation of Ethiopia's religious and artistic heritage.

The art and significance of illuminated manuscripts in the Ethiopian Orthodox tradition are profound. These manuscripts are treasured for their intricate artistry, vibrant colors, and detailed illuminations, which enhance the spiritual and theological messages of the sacred texts. They serve as visual aids that deepen the reader's understanding and meditation on the Bible, making the scriptures more accessible and engaging. The illuminated manuscripts are also invaluable historical documents that provide insights into the religious, cultural, and social life of Ethiopia. They play a crucial role in the transmission and preservation of the Ethiopian Orthodox Bible, ensuring the continuity and accuracy of the biblical texts over generations. The study and appreciation of these manuscripts contribute to the field of art history and foster a deeper understanding of Ethiopia's rich religious and cultural heritage.

# Chapter 19

# Shaping Ethiopian Identity and Spirituality

## The Bible's Enduring Influence on Ethiopian Identity

The Ethiopian Orthodox Bible has profoundly shaped Ethiopian identity over the centuries, intertwining with the nation's cultural, religious, and historical fabric. This influence is evident in various aspects of Ethiopian life, from communal traditions and national celebrations to personal beliefs and social norms. The Bible's role in shaping Ethiopian identity can be traced back to the establishment of Christianity in Ethiopia, which became a cornerstone of Ethiopian civilization.

Christianity was introduced to Ethiopia in the 4th century under the reign of King Ezana of the Aksumite Empire, making it one of the earliest regions to adopt Christianity as a state religion. This early adoption had a lasting impact on Ethiopian identity, establishing a strong connection between the Ethiopian people and the Bible. The Ethiopian Orthodox Church, with its unique canon and liturgical practices, became a central institution in defining Ethiopian religious and cultural life.

The Ethiopian Orthodox Bible's influence is particularly evident in the country's art, literature, and architecture. Ethiopian Christian art, including illuminated manuscripts, iconography, and church frescoes, often reflects biblical themes and figures. These artistic expressions are not merely decorative but serve as a means of conveying religious narratives and teachings. The visual representations of biblical stories in Ethiopian art reinforce the spiritual and cultural significance of the Bible in everyday life.

In literature, the Ethiopian Orthodox Bible has inspired a rich tradition of religious and theological writing. Ethiopian religious texts, hymns, and poetry often draw upon biblical themes and stories. The Bible's influence extends to modern literature as well, where biblical references and motifs can be found in contemporary Ethiopian novels, plays, and poems. This literary engagement with the Bible reflects its continued relevance and impact on Ethiopian cultural expression.

Ethiopian festivals and holidays are deeply rooted in biblical events and themes. Major religious celebrations, such as Timkat (Epiphany), Fasika (Easter), and Meskel (Finding of the True Cross), are not only religious observances but also national events that bring communities together. These festivals often involve processions, feasts, and cultural performances that highlight the Bible's role in shaping Ethiopian communal identity and heritage.

The Bible's influence on Ethiopian identity is also evident in the country's social and moral values. Biblical teachings on justice, compassion, and community service have been integrated into Ethiopian social norms and practices. The concept of "Ubuntu," which emphasizes communal well-being and mutual support, aligns with biblical principles and reflects the ethical teachings of the Bible as they are lived out in Ethiopian society.

The role of the Bible in Ethiopian identity is further manifested in the educational system. Religious education, including the study of the Bible, is an integral part of Ethiopian schooling. From a young age, students are taught biblical stories and moral lessons, which helps to instill a sense of religious and cultural continuity. The Bible serves as a foundational text that shapes the moral and spiritual development of Ethiopian youth.

In times of national crisis or change, the Bible has provided a source of strength and resilience for the Ethiopian people. Historical events such as periods of conflict, political upheaval, and social transformation have often been framed within a biblical context. The Bible's messages of hope, perseverance, and divine providence have offered comfort and guidance during challenging times, reinforcing its role in shaping Ethiopian identity.

The Ethiopian Orthodox Bible's influence extends to religious rituals and ceremonies, which are deeply embedded in Ethiopian cultural practices. For example, the practice of making the sign of the cross, reciting prayers, and performing religious rites are all influenced by biblical teachings. These rituals are not only expressions of faith but also integral components of Ethiopian cultural identity.

The preservation of ancient biblical manuscripts and relics in Ethiopia highlights the enduring importance of the Bible in national heritage. Institutions such as monasteries and churches have played a crucial role in safeguarding these texts, ensuring that the biblical tradition remains a living part of Ethiopian identity. The efforts to preserve and study these manuscripts reflect a deep respect for the Bible's role in Ethiopian history and culture.

The Bible's influence on Ethiopian identity is also evident in the country's unique religious practices and traditions. Ethiopian Christianity has developed distinctive rituals, such as the use of traditional musical instruments in worship and the incorporation of indigenous cultural elements into religious ceremonies. These practices reflect the adaptation of biblical teachings to the local cultural context, creating a distinct Ethiopian expression of Christianity.

The Ethiopian Orthodox Church's role in shaping national identity is further demonstrated through its involvement in public life and social services. The Church has historically played a significant role in education, health care, and social welfare. By providing these services, the Church continues to reflect the Bible's teachings on charity, compassion, and community support, reinforcing its role in Ethiopian society.

The Ethiopian Orthodox Bible has had a profound and enduring influence on Ethiopian identity. Its impact is evident in various aspects of Ethiopian life, including art, literature, festivals, social values, education, and national heritage. The Bible's teachings and narratives have shaped the cultural, moral, and spiritual dimensions of

Ethiopian identity, making it an integral part of the nation's history and cultural expression.

## The Role of Scripture in Ethiopian Spirituality and Religious Practices

The Ethiopian Orthodox Bible is central to the spiritual and religious practices of Ethiopian Orthodox Christians. Its role extends beyond mere textual reference to encompass a wide range of spiritual, ritualistic, and devotional activities. The Bible's teachings and narratives are deeply integrated into the spiritual life of Ethiopian Christians, shaping their practices and beliefs in profound ways.

Daily spiritual practices in Ethiopian Orthodoxy are heavily influenced by biblical scripture. The recitation of psalms, prayers, and hymns is a fundamental part of personal devotion and communal worship. The Psalms, in particular, hold a special place in Ethiopian spirituality. They are recited and chanted at various times throughout the day, reflecting their importance in the daily rhythm of spiritual life.

The liturgical calendar of the Ethiopian Orthodox Church is structured around biblical events and themes. Major feasts and liturgical seasons, such as Advent, Lent, and the Paschal season, are based on the biblical narrative and are celebrated with specific rituals and practices. These liturgical observances provide an opportunity for the faithful to reflect on the central events of the Christian story, including the Incarnation, Crucifixion, and Resurrection of Christ.

The role of scripture in Ethiopian spirituality is also evident in the sacramental life of the Church. The sacraments, or Mysteries, of the Ethiopian Orthodox Church—Baptism, Chrismation, the Eucharist, Confession, Matrimony, and Anointing of the Sick—are all deeply rooted in biblical teachings. For instance, the Eucharist is celebrated with readings from the Gospels and is seen as a direct participation in the sacrificial act of Christ, based on His words at the Last Supper.

In addition to sacramental rites, the Ethiopian Orthodox Church places a strong emphasis on personal and communal prayer. The Bible serves as a guide for these prayers, with specific passages and prayers being used to address various aspects of life and spiritual needs. The use of scripture in prayer helps to anchor personal devotion in the larger biblical narrative and theological framework.

Ethiopian Orthodox monasticism provides another context where the Bible's role in spirituality is evident. Monks and nuns engage in intensive scriptural study, meditation, and prayer as part of their spiritual discipline. The monastic practice of chanting the Psalms and other biblical texts reflects a deep immersion in scripture, aimed at achieving spiritual enlightenment and communion with God.

Biblical scripture also informs the Ethiopian Orthodox approach to spiritual growth and moral conduct. The teachings of the Bible provide ethical guidelines and principles that shape the behavior and attitudes of the faithful. Biblical stories of virtue, repentance, and redemption serve as models for personal and communal life, guiding individuals in their pursuit of holiness and righteousness.

The role of scripture in Ethiopian spirituality is also reflected in the Church's use of icons and religious art. Biblical scenes and figures are depicted in icons, which are used as focal points for meditation and veneration. These visual representations help to bring the biblical narrative to life, allowing the faithful to engage with scripture in a tangible and meaningful way.

In the context of communal worship, scripture is central to the preaching and homilies delivered by clergy. Sermons are based on biblical texts and are intended to provide spiritual guidance, moral teaching, and encouragement to the congregation. The biblical message is thus brought into the everyday lives of the faithful through the homiletic ministry of the Church.

The Ethiopian Orthodox Bible also influences the Church's approach to social and charitable work. Biblical teachings on compassion, justice, and care for the poor and marginalized are reflected in the Church's involvement in social services and humanitarian efforts. The Church's commitment to these values demonstrates the practical application of scripture in addressing social issues and supporting those in need.

The Bible's role in Ethiopian spirituality is also evident in the various religious festivals and processions that are part of Ethiopian Christian life. These celebrations often include readings from the Bible, liturgical hymns, and ritual acts that are inspired by biblical events. The communal aspect of these celebrations reinforces the sense of shared faith and spiritual identity among the faithful.

The Ethiopian Orthodox Bible plays a central role in shaping Ethiopian spirituality and religious practices. Its influence is evident in daily spiritual practices, liturgical observances, sacramental rites, personal and communal prayer, monastic life, ethical conduct, religious art, preaching, social work, and religious festivals. The Bible serves as a foundation for Ethiopian Orthodox spirituality, guiding and enriching the faith and practices of the Ethiopian Christian community.

# Conclusion

The Ethiopian Orthodox Bible represents a profound and enduring legacy within the Ethiopian Orthodox Tewahedo Church and beyond. Its influence extends through various dimensions of Ethiopian life, encompassing religion, culture, and identity. The Bible's deep historical roots in Ethiopia, dating back to the early Christian period, underscore its pivotal role in shaping the spiritual and cultural landscape of the nation. This ancient text continues to serve as a cornerstone of Ethiopian Christianity, preserving a unique tradition that blends biblical teachings with indigenous practices.

The historical significance of the Ethiopian Orthodox Bible is evident in its unique canon and textual tradition. Unlike other Christian traditions, the Ethiopian Orthodox Bible includes several apocryphal and deuterocanonical books that are not found in the canonical scriptures of other denominations. This distinctive feature highlights Ethiopia's rich theological heritage and its commitment to preserving the fullness of biblical revelation as understood within its tradition. The inclusion of these additional texts reflects a broader and more inclusive view of sacred scripture, enriching the religious experience of Ethiopian Orthodox Christians.

The role of the Bible in Ethiopian liturgical practices is equally significant. The Ethiopian Orthodox Church's liturgical calendar, with its rich array of feasts, fasts, and celebrations, is deeply rooted in biblical events and themes. These liturgical observances provide a framework for spiritual growth and communal worship, reinforcing the Bible's central place in the life of the Church. The integration of biblical texts into liturgical rituals, sacraments, and daily prayers ensures that the scriptures remain a living and dynamic part of Ethiopian Christian practice.

The art and illumination of Ethiopian biblical manuscripts further demonstrate the Bible's impact on Ethiopian culture. The intricate and vibrant artwork found in these manuscripts reflects a deep reverence for the sacred texts and a commitment to preserving their beauty and significance. The illuminated manuscripts serve not only as objects of artistic and historical value but also as expressions of spiritual devotion and theological insight. The rich visual tradition of Ethiopian manuscript illumination continues to inspire admiration and scholarly study.

Ethiopian identity and spirituality are profoundly shaped by the Bible. The integration of biblical teachings into Ethiopian social values, cultural practices, and religious rituals underscores the Bible's role in defining and expressing Ethiopian Christian identity. From personal devotions and communal celebrations to national festivals and moral conduct, the Bible influences every aspect of Ethiopian life. Its teachings provide a foundation for ethical behavior, spiritual growth, and communal solidarity.

The preservation and digitization efforts surrounding Ethiopian biblical manuscripts highlight the ongoing commitment to safeguarding this invaluable heritage. The projects aimed at preserving and making these manuscripts accessible to a global audience demonstrate a recognition of their historical and cultural importance. By ensuring the long-term preservation of these texts and making them available for study and appreciation, these efforts contribute to the continued relevance of the Ethiopian Orthodox Bible in the modern world.

In the realm of scholarly research, the Ethiopian Orthodox Bible offers rich insights into early Christian history, biblical textual criticism, and theological development. The study of Ethiopian biblical manuscripts provides valuable information about the transmission of biblical texts, the evolution of Christian doctrine, and the interaction of religious traditions. Scholars of religion, history, and culture benefit from the unique perspectives offered by the Ethiopian Bible, enhancing their understanding of the broader Christian and historical context.

The Bible's role in Ethiopian spirituality is deeply ingrained in daily life and religious practices. The recitation of psalms, participation in sacraments, and engagement in liturgical rituals are all informed by biblical teachings. The Bible's influence extends beyond formal worship to encompass personal and communal prayer, moral guidance, and spiritual development. The integration of scripture into various aspects of Ethiopian Christian practice underscores its centrality in shaping and sustaining the faith.

The Ethiopian Orthodox Bible's impact on Ethiopian culture is evident in the country's artistic, literary, and social traditions. The biblical narratives and teachings have inspired a rich body of religious art, literature, and music that reflects the deep connection between scripture and cultural expression. The ongoing relevance of these artistic and literary traditions demonstrates the Bible's enduring influence on Ethiopian identity and heritage.

The global recognition and appreciation of Ethiopian biblical manuscripts and traditions underscore the significance of the Ethiopian Orthodox Bible in the broader Christian and scholarly communities. The efforts to showcase Ethiopian biblical heritage through exhibitions, publications, and digital platforms highlight the universal value of these texts and their contributions to the global understanding of Christian history and culture.

The Ethiopian Orthodox Bible represents a profound and enduring legacy that continues to shape Ethiopian identity, spirituality, and cultural expression. Its unique textual tradition, liturgical significance, artistic heritage, and scholarly importance underscore its central role in Ethiopian Christianity. The ongoing efforts to preserve, study, and share this invaluable heritage ensure that the Bible's influence will persist for future generations, contributing to the rich tapestry of global Christian history and cultural heritage.

The Ethiopian Orthodox Bible and its associated traditions remain profoundly relevant in the contemporary world. Despite the challenges and changes faced by Ethiopian Christianity over the centuries, the core teachings and practices rooted in this ancient scripture continue to resonate with the faithful. The

Bible's enduring significance is reflected in the vibrant religious life of the Ethiopian Orthodox Tewahedo Church and its impact on Ethiopian culture and identity.

The continued relevance of Ethiopian Orthodox tradition is evident in the ongoing practice of liturgical rites and rituals that are deeply rooted in biblical teachings. The Ethiopian Orthodox Church's commitment to preserving traditional liturgical practices, such as the celebration of the Divine Liturgy and the observance of major feasts, underscores the Bible's central role in shaping worship and spiritual life. These practices connect the faithful with a rich heritage of Christian worship that has been passed down through generations.

The Ethiopian Orthodox Church's dedication to maintaining its unique canon of scripture and theological teachings also reflects the enduring relevance of its traditions. The inclusion of additional biblical texts and the distinctive theological perspectives of Ethiopian Orthodoxy offer a broader and more inclusive view of Christian doctrine. This commitment to preserving and interpreting these texts in accordance with Ethiopian tradition ensures that the Bible remains a living and dynamic source of spiritual guidance.

The influence of Ethiopian Orthodox traditions extends beyond the boundaries of Ethiopia. The global recognition of Ethiopian biblical manuscripts, religious art, and cultural practices highlights the universal significance of Ethiopian Christian heritage. The efforts to share and celebrate these traditions on the international stage contribute to a broader understanding of Christian diversity and the rich tapestry of global religious heritage.

In the realm of education and scholarship, the continued study of Ethiopian biblical manuscripts and traditions provides valuable insights into the development of early Christian thought and practice. The scholarly examination of these texts and their historical context contributes to a deeper understanding of Christian history and theology. The ongoing research and publications related to Ethiopian Orthodox tradition ensure that its significance is acknowledged and appreciated within the academic community.

The role of Ethiopian Orthodox traditions in shaping personal and communal spirituality remains a key aspect of their continued relevance. The integration of biblical teachings into daily life, personal devotions, and communal worship continues to provide a source of inspiration and guidance for Ethiopian Orthodox Christians. The Bible's teachings on morality, compassion, and community support are lived out through these practices, reinforcing the relevance of scripture in contemporary spiritual life.

The preservation and promotion of Ethiopian Orthodox traditions also contribute to cultural continuity and identity. The celebration of religious festivals, the production of religious art, and the maintenance of traditional practices all serve to strengthen a sense of cultural heritage and communal belonging. These traditions help to foster a strong connection to the past while addressing the spiritual needs of the present.

The ongoing efforts to digitize and make Ethiopian biblical manuscripts accessible to a global audience further underscore the relevance of these traditions in the modern world. By making these texts available for study and appreciation, these initiatives ensure that the rich heritage of Ethiopian Orthodox Christianity can be shared with a wider audience. This global engagement helps to preserve and promote the importance of Ethiopian biblical tradition on the international stage.

In the context of interfaith dialogue and ecumenical relations, the Ethiopian Orthodox Bible and its traditions offer valuable perspectives on the diversity of Christian experience. The unique theological and liturgical practices of Ethiopian Orthodoxy contribute to a broader understanding of Christian faith and practice, enriching the dialogue between different Christian traditions. This engagement fosters mutual respect and appreciation for the diversity of Christian heritage.

The relevance of Ethiopian Orthodox traditions is also reflected in the ongoing commitment to social and charitable work. The teachings of the Bible on justice, compassion, and service continue to inspire the Ethiopian Orthodox Church's involvement in humanitarian efforts and community support. This commitment to addressing social issues and supporting those in need reflects the practical application of biblical principles in contemporary life.

The Ethiopian Orthodox Bible and its associated traditions remain profoundly relevant in the contemporary world. The continued practice of liturgical rites, the preservation of unique theological perspectives, and the global recognition of Ethiopian Christian heritage all underscore the enduring significance of these traditions. The ongoing engagement with Ethiopian Orthodox traditions in education, scholarship, spirituality, and social work ensures that their relevance will persist for future generations, contributing to the rich and diverse tapestry of global Christian heritage.